The
Router Joinery
Handbook

The Router Joinery Handbook

Innovative jigs, fixtures and techniques for creating flawless joints every time

Pat Warner

POPULAR WOODWORKING BOOKS
CINCINNATI, OHIO

02 01 00 99 98   5   4   3   2   1

Library of Congress Cataloging-in-Publication Data

Warner, Pat.
    The router joinery handbook / Pat Warner.—1st ed.
        p.   cm.
    Includes index.
    ISBN 1-55870-444-2 (alk. paper)
    1. Routers (Tools)—Handbooks, manuals, etc. 2.
Woodwork—Handbooks, manuals, etc. 3. Joinery—
Handbooks, manuals, etc. I. Title.
TT203.5.W374   1998
684'.08—dc21   97-26370
                                              CIP

Edited by R. Adam Blake
Content edited by Bruce E. Stoker
Production edited by Amy Jeynes
Designed by Kathy DeZarn and Brian Roeth
Cover designed by Chad Planner

DISCLAIMER

To prevent accidents, keep safety in mind while you work. Use the safety guards installed on power equipment; they are for your protection. When working on power equipment, keep fingers away from saw blades, wear safety goggles to prevent injuries from flying wood chips and sawdust, wear ear protection to protect your hearing, and consider installing a dust vacuum to reduce the amount of airborne sawdust in your woodshop. Don't wear loose clothing, such as neckties or shirts with loose sleeves, or jewelry, such as rings, necklaces or bracelets, when working on power equipment, and tie back long hair to prevent it from getting caught in your equipment. People who are sensitive to certain chemicals should check the chemical content of any product before using it. The author and editors who compiled this book have tried to make all the contents as accurate and correct as possible. Plans, illustrations, photographs and text have been carefully checked. All instructions, plans and projects should be carefully read, studied and understood before beginning construction. Due to the variability of local conditions, construction materials, skill levels, etc., neither the author nor Popular Woodworking Books assumes any responsibility for any accidents, injuries, damages or other losses incurred resulting from the material presented in this book.

METRIC CONVERSION CHART		
TO CONVERT	**TO**	**MULTIPLY BY**
Inches	Centimeters	2.54
Centimeters	Inches	0.4
Feet	Centimeters	30.5
Centimeters	Feet	0.03
Yards	Meters	0.9
Meters	Yards	1.1
Sq. Inches	Sq. Centimeters	6.45
Sq. Centimeters	Sq. Inches	0.16
Sq. Feet	Sq. Meters	0.09
Sq. Meters	Sq. Feet	10.8
Sq. Yards	Sq. Meters	0.8
Sq. Meters	Sq. Yards	1.2
Pounds	Kilograms	0.45
Kilograms	Pounds	2.2
Ounces	Grams	28.4
Grams	Ounces	0.04

ABOUT THE AUTHOR

The clay sculptor has the ideal opportunity to contend with any of his mistakes. The malleability of his material allows for an infinite number of remedies at little expense or risk to the project. The woodworker, on the other hand, has only two choices when presented with an error. He can make the workpiece over or change the work to suit the mishap; both options are likely to involve compromise. The key, then, is getting it right the first time.

My nature is to make mistakes. I'm not one to get it right on the first go-around. Notwithstanding, if I do it more than once I usually do it better each time. Twenty-three years of self-taught woodworking has been one long series of mistakes. However, since I've screwed up so many times in so many ways I've become pretty good at what I do.

My education was in the sciences and therefore I have learned and I've been blessed with excellent observational skills. This combination of hands-on experience and a keen sense of the task make it easy for me to know when something is apt to go wrong. And, when I'm in uncharted territory I'm only half as likely to blow it.

As a furniture designer/craftsman I've designed and made hundreds of pieces. I'm skilled in case goods and sleepware and I'm no stranger to benches, desks, tables and seating. I've made all my jigs and fixtures and I've made a few on commission. My primary tool has been and still is the router. I use a dozen or so for ordinary work and I often apply them to tasks most woodworkers would find strange or at the very least serendipitous. I do all my joinery with routers, I joint all stock edges on one, and, of couse, all my template and pattern work is router cut.

I've been called on by the router bit and router manufacturing industry to consult from time to time and I teach routing at the Palomar Community College in San Marcos, California. I am the inventor of the Acrylic Offset Router Sub-Base and I make the accessory for the Porter Cable Corporation and DeWalt Industrial Tool Company. Incidentally my sub-base is hand fabricated with an assortment of twin-pin, table and hand routers using seven different cutters.

My routing experience has been helpful and of some interest to the readers of many current publications including *Fine Woodworking*, *American Woodworker*, and *Woodwork* magazines. I am a contributing editor for *Woodwork*.

ACKNOWLEDGMENTS

I would like to thank the following people for their help in making this an interesting and worthwhile book: J.A. Warner, artist Terry Kirkpatrick for most of the drawings and Jürgen Amtmann for his engineering advice. If this book turns out to be a success, Adam Blake deserves the lion's share of the credit, as he knew where the weaknesses in the manuscript were, how to fix them and how to inspire the author without intimidating him. (If the book blows up, we'll blame him for that too.) Chuck Hicks of Whiteside Machinery, Brian Corbley of Amana Tool Corp., Carlo Venditto of Jesada Tools, Inc., and Patrick Spielman are the router bit experts from whom I often sought help. I'd also like to thank Carter Williams of DeWalt, Leslie Banduch of Porter Cable, Ken Grisley and his son of Leigh Industries, John Goff, Colonel Joe Kirkpatrick, Mike Roten of Woodworkers' Supply, Richard Wedler of Microfence, Al and Joan Weiss, Barry Rundstrom of PRC, Nathan Warner, Dida Warner, Nan Bushley and Eric Johnson.

Once again, Ken Schroeder deserves a special thanks for most of the printing of the photos and frequent advice to me on just how to light, compose and shoot film. He knows only excellence. Photo credit also belongs to Brian Allen of L.S. Starret, Leigh Industries, Dave Keller, Porter Cable, Jointech, Taylor Design Group, Inc. and C.B. Wilson, M.D. for figures 1-1, 1-3, 1-4, 1-5A and 1-5B.

This book is dedicated to
my son, Derek George Warner.

TABLE OF CONTENTS

TABLE OF CONTENTS (CONTINUED)

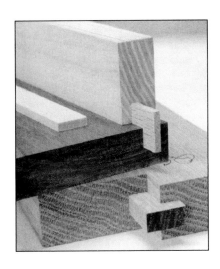

INTRODUCTION

Joinery is the practice of fastening boards to one another. Some joints, such as those from China and Japan, can be so intrusive and sophisticated as to require no glue, show no end grain and last for centuries. On the other hand, joints can be made quite simply. For example, butt joints, shear panels, dowels, nails, plastic knockdown hardware and corrugated fasteners are the typical connections in upholstered furniture and production kitchen cabinets. These too can last a long time.

The point is, joinery and assembly are diverse, and their sophistication (or lack of it) doesn't necessarily determine the life or service of a given piece of woodwork. To further illustrate, let's take a typical rail-and-stile configuration. If the components of this assembly are sufficiently strong and appropriately joined with through-tenons and wedges, the assembly will be quite rigid and serviceable. It might even survive the rigors of schoolchildren or the impact of a prison riot. The same four sticks lightly basted together but covered on both sides with ¼"-thick sheets of exterior plywood and glued can be equally durable, although perhaps not as interesting.

You may have a dollhouse to make by Christmas or a Stickley re-creation for a fussy client. Whatever the case, the choices in joinery and assembly of furniture and cabinets are wide judgment calls and not really the subject of this book. Learning just where and when to use a particular joint is very complicated. If you make a lot of stuff, attend enough classes, go to the galleries and exhibitions and read like crazy, in time you'll be a good joiner. It doesn't come overnight and, as you know, anything worthwhile ain't easy.

As a woodworker, you have maybe four avenues to choose from in learning the practice of joinery and assembly. You can learn the entire process using only hand tools. You can also do much of the work with just machine tools. You may choose not to facet (cut) any of your joinery, and instead nail-gun, hot-glue and shear-panel your cabinets together. Finally, you can design, cut and assemble using techniques from all three schools of thought. If you decide to use some machine tool processes, and in particular the electric router, you'll like this book.

For a long time I've been joining my furniture and case goods using routers and handmade jigs and fixtures. Routers aren't very useful without some sort of jig to hold, index and offer guidance and support to either the work or the router. In fact, jigs are essential in cutting all the joints in this book. I will describe the jigs, their construction and their capacities in detail. In addition, whenever I thought the capacity might be compromised, those dimensions of the jig that control capacity are indicated, so you can easily make the tool bigger or smaller to suit your needs without redesigning the whole thing.

I don't claim to have the last word in router joinery; there are plenty of people out there with more skill and talent than I. My joining systems, however, have evolved in the shop and have stood the tests of hard use and time. You may even consider my jigs and fixtures more of a challenge than the joints they allow you to cut. Notwithstanding, if you give the jig the attention it deserves, you will be pleasantly surprised at the results and at just how safely and quickly you can cut joints.

Although the router is unparalleled in its range of capabilities, it does have its limitations, and you cannot expect to do much at the extremes. For instance, the cutters for long, narrow dovetails are either too fragile or nonexistent. And the joinery encountered in timber framing is of such a scale that the router has neither the power nor the prowess to be of much help. The joinery in this book is suitable for a 1½ hp router and well within its power and safety zones. My first book, *Getting the Very Best From Your Router* (Betterway, 1996), puts this concept into perspective. If you need more information on basic routery, including selection, range and safe operation of routers, *Getting the Very Best From Your Router* is time and money well spent. *The Router Joinery Handbook* is devoted to the nuts and bolts of ordinary—and some extraordinary—router joinery.

CHAPTER ONE
Why Use a Router for Joinery?

There are countless ways of making and joining the parts from a cutting list into a woodworking project. If you work by hand, you have the full western joinery repertoire at your disposal. Having that range of capability, however, doesn't come easy: The training required can take years, and the opportunity to learn those skills is rapidly reaching the point of extinction.

Router joinery, on the other hand, can be picked up pretty easily, and the joints I've cov-ered in this book can be applied to a wide range of furniture- and cabinet-making applications. Due to the nature of routing and the cutters themselves, however, the range of router work will always fall short of what the hand-joiner can do, primarily because a router can't saw. Thin-line saw wasting and narrow chisel work cannot be duplicated with routers. There are no cutters for such work, and routers are just not very good at cutting too far away from their last armature bearing (collet).

Figure 1-1

My credenza is an experimental piece. I tried a lot of new things in it including the stand and the slid-ing frame-and-panel doors, and the dove-tails were cut into the box after glue-up! I couldn't have made it without my routers.

ROUTERS ARE FLEXIBLE

It is, however, absolutely astounding to see just what can be made within these limitations. The credenza in Figure 1-1, dovetails and all, was largely router-made. All the surfaces were tongued and grooved, the doors were mortised and tenoned, and the stand is joined with sliding dovetails and joint-connector bolts.

My oak chair (Figure 1-2) was entirely router-cut. In fact, the stock was routed round from rectangular material after assembly. The seat was glue-jointed and the spindles were tenoned on my tenon jig.

The legal-size file box (Figure 1-3) was another router challenge. The stand is 6/4 white oak with a series of shallow but definite details routed into it. Its mortises and tenons were all router-cut. The drawers, drawer handles, top and back were all routed at relatively shallow depths with standard cutters.

The sharp details in the off-end view of my desk (where I wrote this book) were all the result of routings produced with off-the-shelf cutters. I had to make plenty of templates and jigs but the router was with me all the way (Figure 1-4).

And finally, the office desk (Figures 1-5A

Figure 1-2

My chair was also an experiment. My intention was to copy the simplicity and look of bent steel tubing in wood. All the rounding was router-cut—no stick was ever in a lathe.

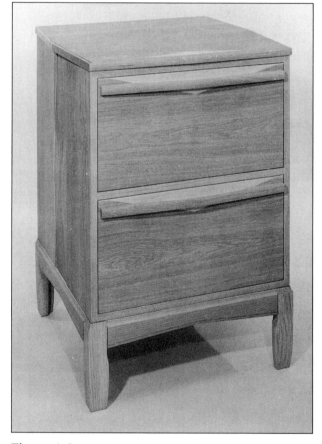

Figure 1-3

The tongue-and-groove paneling, the sliding dovetail drawer construction and the tenoning and mortising of the legs and rails in this cabinet will be covered in later chapters.

Figure 1-4

The sliding dovetail is the key element to the integrity of the end assembly of my desk.

and B) is another example of just what a router can do. None of the cuts you see are very extensive. If you just keep at it, there isn't much you can't make or join with a router.

Router joinery is indeed an important and rewarding part of the woodworking process. One of the reasons for this success is the router's intrusive behavior. It can approach nearly any spot on a workpiece, even ones often not accessible with other power equipment.

ROUTER JOINERY IS VERSATILE

Joinery is challenging because of the enormous possibilities of two or more sticks meeting one another (Figures 1-6A–D). Let's take an ordinary cabinet. Boards are first joined edge to edge to form panels. The end of one of these panels may join the face of another as a shelf. A new panel

Figure 1-5A

This six-drawer pedestal desk uses router joinery throughout. The Koa inserted into the top is a full-thickness tongue-and-groove complementary template operation. The T&G was the perfect joint to register the Koa in its oak residence.

Figure 1-5B

This detail shows a rabbeted dovetail (case corner), a routed drawer pull and a routed decorative excavation in the drawer front.

may link up with the end of that one to form a top. An apron can be applied under the top and into the cabinet sides to balance the design and stiffen the assembly; a rabbeted or tongued back will add to the project's integrity too. Drawers, drawer blades, dividers and doors are also potential elements in the structure, each with its own set of positional and joinery peculiarities. In ev-

ery case, a router, perhaps an attendant jig, and the router bit can access the site and execute the cuttings at the joint interface. Moreover, a router bit can access an edge, an end or the face of a board; its cut can be blind, fractional or full thickness. The router is the perfect tool for access and joinery: No other single electric tool has these capabilities.

Figure 1-6A
This double tongue-and-groove was cut entirely on the router table with a ¼" slotter. This joint is useful for making thick material from skinny stock.

Figure 1-6B
A glue joint like this one could be used to join boards edge to edge or edge to face, or even to join drawer sides to fronts.

Figure 1-6C
This experimental joint was created from a series of cutters and templates. I designed the joint for maximum pull strength. I wanted a lap so I could take it apart.

Figure 1-6D
This shallow but attractive joint requires a fastener to keep it together. This joint would usually require twin tenons for a strong connection, but the bolt is even better. If the connection ever loosens, a twist of the bolt cinches it right up.

A ROUTER ADAPTS WELL TO JIGS AND FIXTURES

Success in joinery can also be attributed to the router's simple design and its acceptance of ready-made and handmade jig and fixture helpers. Aside from sophisticated system router machinery like the WoodRat, Multi-Router, Strong Machine or the Match-Maker, consider for a moment the number of commercially made router joinery accessories. Porter Cable, for one, makes the Morten, Tru-Match, Omnijig and a whole series of edge and collar guides. Dovetail template jigs of all sorts, as well as incremental and continuously adjustable router-table fences, are everywhere. Cope and stick cutters (ready to join door stiles and rails) are in virtually every cutter catalog, as are glue and finger joint bits (Figure 1-7). Later on we'll investigate a mortiser, a tenon-making jig and some easy-to-make sliding dovetail fixtures made by and designed for routers. Routers, cutters, jigs and fixtures all lend themselves to the art of joinery.

Figure 1-7
All these cutters are designed for joinery. They are adaptable to many different workpiece sizes and the same cutter often has more than one joinery application.

ROUTER BITS AND JOINERY

Besides the obvious job-specific joiner bits (dovetails and glue joints, for example), router bits are indeed novel and well matched to the task of joinery. All joints are excavations of length, depth and width. A router bit can slice and pare equally well on the side or the bottom of its cutting flutes. The finish of the walls and floor of a dado or dovetail way, for example, cut with a well-made bit, will be indistinguishable.

A circular saw blade can never do that, nor will most hand tools. Most saw-cut joinery is overlapped such that each new cut is clearly etched into the stock. Hammer-and-chisel–cut joinery is always obvious, although as one's skill level increases, the cosmetics of the work improve. Joiner, rabbet and molding planes are notable exceptions and can indeed produce near-perfect surfaces; however, their control, adjustment and sharpening can take considerable skill. A piloted carbide rabbet bit in a medium-size router, on the other hand, can produce impeccable results even in the hands of a novice.

ROUTER JOINERY OFFERS SIMPLICITY AND ECONOMY

Up until the time of the latest woodworking renaissance (the mid-1970s), cabinet and furniture joinery was largely either shaper-cut or done with hand tools. Both systems have their advantages, but a few things really stand out here. Shaper work is expensive and generally for the production run; it is also done at some expense to the design of a product, since inside cuttings (like mortises) are not possible on a shaper.

Handwork, on the other hand, has no boundaries. Both inside and outside cuts are possible, as are cuttings along the insides or outsides of curves. The referencing problems so critical in shaper work are substantially simplified for the hand-tool craftsman. Hand tools are also generally much cheaper than electric machinery and last a lot longer, but they do require considerable practice and skill to use well. Hand-worked joinery is also confined today to the nonproduction environment.

Now, enter the router, a revolution in itself. Its design is so simple that (with a few jigs and a couple of guides and straight bits) mortises, tenons, tongues, grooves, laps and box joints are now possible. The introduction of the plunge router simplified the multiple-depth inside cuttings like mortises, and a little tungsten carbide on the bit allows us to cut for extended periods without burning out the tool. Then, with the thoughtful design and evolution of such tools as the dovetail template, edge guide and the router table, the production environment was entered—and the rest is history.

Today the price of a medium-grade commercial router is around $150; straight bits are made in such quantity that they cost nearly the same as an all-steel bit of the 1980s. The economies of routing are so obvious that the router is now the second most abundant electric tool in North America, often replacing the shaper that preceded it.

ROUTER JOINERY IS EASY TO LEARN

Hand tools are not perfect; however, the experienced hand-tool craftsman can produce joints of acceptable to outstanding quality. But the skills and time required to do outstanding work can be considerable. The nature of wood is just too variable to be knifed away with hand tools with any predictability. For example, a chisel or saw

blade may lock onto a dense growth ring and steer your tool away from the scribe line. Overcoming the strangeness of species-sensitive characteristics, grain and annual ring nuances can be challenging and is one of the hallmarks of the true hand-tool craftsman.

The router woodworker shares some of these problems with the materials, but with sharp tooling and the overwhelming power advantage of an electric tool, the problems are greatly reduced. Furthermore, there are no freehand router joinery cuts: All joint excavations are controlled cuts. The operator merely has to determine how much material to waste and how fast. This takes some practice and perhaps a little talent, but routed dovetails and box joints can be learned in a day or two. Precision hand-cut joinery can take years.

ROUTING JOINTS IS FAST AND ACCURATE

Essentially, every router-cut joint is controlled. The depth, length and width of the cut are con-

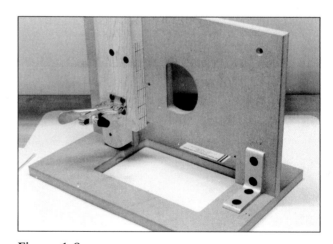

Figure 1-8

This tenon-making jig can index and position the work in under 30". The window size and the fence location allow stock up to 6" wide and 6/4 thick to be tenoned. The work can be of any practical length.

trolled by such things as the cutter extension, an edge or collar guide, template, bearing, fence or some such contrivance. The art of router joinery is really just organizing and selecting the hardware to waste wood away. The setup is as quick as your jigs and cutters are efficient. If your jigs are simple and apply themselves well to all sizes of stock, the setups are quick. For example, the tenon setup in Figure 1-8 can be arranged in under 30 seconds for very thin stock up to 6/4 × 6″. The cut is often just as quick; in fact, it usually takes less time than the setup.

The accuracy of the cuttings is under your control. The hand-tool craftsman often uses depth-limiting tools, but just as frequently he has to cut to a knife or other scribe line. Working to the waste side of the line takes some skill and a good eye. The same problems confront the router operator, but the setup can be measured to any degree of accuracy before the cut. Moreover, the cutter's pathway is predetermined, and that element of the operation involves very little risk. The hand tooler, on the other hand, is often cutting with only his skill and experience and depends on acute hand-eye coordination. Don't get me wrong—I have the highest regard for those who have chosen to learn hand skills. My temperament is such that I prefer a faster result, less training and less chance of error—all of which can be found with a router.

ROUTING JOINTS IS FUN!

Routing joints can be fun, especially when the boundaries of the joint are not realized until the final pass (Figure 1-9). Mortises and tenons are similar in this respect. The tenons I make while the workpiece is on end are not evident until the bearing on the cutter contacts the edges and faces of the stock. While the cutter is paring

Figure 1-9
The incomplete tenon cut on the left is simply useless—and ugly at that. When the bearing on the cutter meets the face and edges of the stock a crisp tenon emerges as if by magic.

Figure 1-10
Though you may not realize it, most routing is "freehand"! The first phase of the cutting in this mortise (left) has been cut with the stops and slides out-of-play. Seconds later, as the base casting slides against its stops and the edge guide is against the work, the mortise becomes well defined (right).

away the material to "get at" the tenon, you'd never guess such a work of art would emerge. The same thing happens with the mortise.

My mortises are cut in a fixture with two edge guides and stops for travel north and south. My approach is to plunge the tool bit into the center of the mortise and work the router toward the extension of the guides and stops. This attack puts the stress on the cutter where it matters the least—in the center of the mortise. As the cutter approaches the walls of the mortise, it takes less and less wood; hence there is a diminishing stress on the cutter. The result is a mortise with very clean walls (see Figure 1-10). A viewing of the work in progress always shows a random messy excavation, but during the last pass a well-defined mortise appears as if by magic. Every time I make the cut, it's fun.

A ROUTER CAN BE A DEDICATED OR SUPPLEMENTAL TOOL

The router is my primary joining tool; it may not become yours. You may be dedicated to your jointer, shaper, saw or hand tools. And I'm the first to admit the router is not for everybody. Whatever the case may be, I'd like you to consider a few things in favor of routing joints.

Most tools are designed to do a few things well. A jointer can rabbet, but its main task is truing surfaces. A table saw can cut tenons, slots and risky mortises, but it really saws up stuff to width and length quite nicely. The shaper can edge- and glue-joint well, but it can't mortise or dovetail. The router isn't perfect either, but overall it does more things and does them better than any other tool.

For those of you who must dado with a table saw or mortise with a chisel, may I suggest you augment that dedicated practice with a few light cuts from a router. There is no question that small rabbets and tongues are most expeditiously and precisely done with a router. If you cut away most of the waste of a rabbet on your table saw and finish the cut with a router, you'll get a much better result than with a table saw alone. Ditto with dados (Figure 1-11). A light cut with a straight bit and guide can render your saw-serrated dados as crisp as if they were laser-cut. The point I'm trying to make is that a choice from column A (e.g., your table saw) and one from column B (the router) may add up to more than just A + B. Exploit the efficiencies you're now skilled in, but add a little routing when it makes sense.

Figure 1-11

Both samples are dadoed. (The sample on the left was table-sawn.) Those skilled on the table saw can usually get good results; I can't. The broader cut was hand-routed. The sawn sample can be identified by the saw tooth marks on the floor of the slot. There are no discernible mill marks on the routed sample.

CHAPTER TWO

Router Joinery Basics

DIMENSIONING AND SQUARING YOUR STOCK

Joinery is a two-step process. The first step is sizing the material; the second is the actual cutting of the joint. If the joinery process is not considered in this way, you will have problems in "fitting."

A workpiece to be joined can be referenced from the stock itself or from a jig that is referenced from the stock (Figure 2-1). In either case, good dimensioning is essential. Dimensioning

Figure 2-1
The position of the adjustable template on this jig is not referenced from the work. The template is part of the jig. The template is parallel to the work and does travel that way, however.

must be under your control in order to achieve acceptable and consistent results. If you don't have the machinery or the skills to size up your stock, consider having this work done professionally.

Dimensioning can be divided into two parts, each equally important. A board to be joined must not only be of the correct size, with all of its edges and corners at the correct angles, but it has to be free of any major defects such as bow, twist or cup. Bow, twist and cup are expressions of stress. They may occur because of a poor drying schedule or perhaps as a result of the tree's life history. The tree may have grown on a hill that slumped during its growth, or it may have been blown from only one direction. Competition for sun and water may have produced branches or roots that favor one side of the tree or the other. Whatever the cause, distorted wood is difficult to reference from and can be hazardous to machine. In my estimation, more than half of the stock we use is stress wood. When I prepare stock for joinery, I'm aware that stress relief can show up after each cutting operation. Joining and planing are not particularly the culprits here, since these are truing operations and remove relatively little stock. Sawing, on the other hand, radically modifies lumber to the extent that one flat stick, on occasion, can turn into two crooked ones. To cope with this problem, I first rough (band) saw my lumber into boards near their finished dimensions, and then machine the boards in the conventional way: jointing them flat, planing to thickness, ripping to width and crosscutting to length.

Using the Jointer

The jointer flattens and edges stock. It is more economical and physically easier to joint stock that is as near to finished size as possible. A rough-sawn unmilled board is not particularly safe to cut up into small pieces and joint, but it can be managed satisfactorily with a jigsaw or band saw. I usually rough-saw my material before jointing it.

Joint the face of your stock until it is flat. Use a machined surface such as a table casting or jointer bed to compare for flatness. You can also use a machinist's square or a ground straightedge to verify or rule out cup and twist, respectively. If the finished thickness is more than ¼″ away, I usually joint the opposite face as well. Keep in mind the faces will not be parallel, but it's a good idea to remove equal amounts of stock from both sides to maintain stability within the stock. Before planing, joint one or both edges. You should now have a stick that is flat on one or both sides, not necessarily of uniform thickness, and with one or both of its long-grain edges square to one face. The edge(s) should be straight as well as square. I'll often verify the straightness against the jointer fence, or I'll use a ground straightedge.

It is at this point that I decide whether to rough rip again or just throw the whole board into the planer. My decision is based on whether I can handle the board adequately and what I estimate the stress to be. The closer your stock is to finished size as you joint and plane, the less

change in shape you're likely to encounter as you progress to the table saw. As a rule I saw to within ⅛″ of finished width before planing.

Planing Your Stock

The planer planes a board to a uniform thickness. Since I usually pre-joint both faces of the lumber I use, it's easy to lose track of which face I'm planing. When both faces are jointed, I pencil across the width of one side five or ten times down the length of the board to monitor the progress of the planer. Once that face is completely planed (all pencil lines are gone), subsequent passes are on opposite faces until the final thickness is achieved.

Planing is a critical process: Uniform thickness is essential to good joinery. Safe router joinery requires you to reference off both faces of the board. If your stock is not parallel and uniform in thickness, the joint members (of either sex) will not be of uniform thickness nor breadth; consequently, your joints will either jam, rattle or wedge. I try to maintain a thickness tolerance of ±.002″ across and down the full length of the workpiece. This may seem extreme, but most planers can do this without any heroics. Remember: A major source of poor-fitting joints is bad milling, and improper planing in particular. Incidentally, if you usually hand-plane your material, you will have to pass the stock through a thickness planer at least once on one side, as it is nearly impossible to uniformly thickness a board by hand to ±.002″.

In the literature this aspect of joinery is either not stressed or omitted, and it is true that satisfactory joinery is possible with ill-prepared stock. The trick is to rout while referencing from only one side of the board (the reference surface is the surface that you machine or mark from). Routing this way, however, brings with it certain hazards, as inevitably the cutter will become trapped between the work and the guide. (The guide might be a template, a fence or an edge guide.) Believe me, it is much easier and safer to accept the fact that your boards have to be planed flat, even and square than it is to work with lesser material. Deviations from these standards have a way of causing a cascade of problems as you progress through your work.

Edge Planing the Stock

Edge planing is the same as face planing (the previous step) except the stock is fed to the cutters on edge. It is an accurate and usually safe way to bring a board to uniform width without sawing. If the stock I'm preparing is more than ⅞″ thick and less than 4″ wide, I consider edge plan-

ing. Stock out of this range is too risky to plane in my planer. Use common sense and follow the manufacturer's recommendations; this is not a common practice on skinny stock.

Rip Sawing to Width

After joining and planing, the boards should be ripped to final width. "Ripped to width" is the vernacular for parallelism, or making the sides parallel. If your boards are nearly to final width when they reach this stage, the ripping process will produce a minimum of new distortion. Sawing wide, long boards into short, narrow ones frequently produces a lot of misshapen stock. Be prepared for this. A sawn edge produced from a good blade and fed at a uniform rate is as a rule acceptable for router joinery.

TRAPPED CUTTER

The trapped-cutter condition occurs when a cutter is confined to an area where it has no safe escape route. Most outside-bearing-guided cuts are not hazardous. The bearing limits the cross–lateral travel of the cutter, and you can always drive the router out and away from the edge without consequence. On the router table, a dovetail cutter (Figure 2-2) on the face away from the fence has the work trapped between it and the cutter. Any deviation in the control of the workpiece spells "curtains" for the work, and the cutter may break from an unexpected and instantaneous high stress. The cutter simply has no safe haven; it is trapped by the position of the fence. Pay attention to all your setups to ensure that this condition never occurs. Think through the cutting process before starting so your hands are always clear of the cutter.

Figure 2-2
Here, the cutter is positioned on the outside of the stock only as an illustration of what not to do. Work fed this way can self-feed, kick back, or God knows what.

CROSSCUTTING AND SANDING

The final stage of milling is the crosscut. A table saw crosscut is usually superior to a radial or chop saw slice, although that is debatable. Most woodworking processes from here on will reference off these cuts. Router joinery may be a little more sensitive to square cuts than other machinery. Make sure your end cuts are square to the edges and faces of the board, and that you're consistent. On critical cuts, I sand the end grain square on my edge sander, as a lot of indexing errors are traceable to a lousy end cut.

INDEXING YOUR WORK

Indexing is the process of locating or nesting a workpiece in a fixture (holder) in a predictable and repeatable way (Figure 2-3). In much the same way, it can also refer to the act of locating stuff (jigs, guides and such) on the work (Figure 2-4). Either way, if your material is poorly milled, misshapen or out of square, indexing is reduced to mere guessing, and a guess here can produce only variable results. If your stock is

Figure 2-4
I can locate the template in the same place every time with this simple rabbeted stick.

Figure 2-5
The arrow on the end grain signifies not only the reference end of the stick and its number in the sequence, but it also points to the face side of the board.

milled to above-average standards, you can rule this out as a source of error—and believe me, anything can be a source of error in joinery. Minor discrepancies in workpiece geometry can be compensated for by referencing off the common ends, edges or faces of the assembly. This should be the normal way of doing woodwork, regardless of how well you mill.

Before laying out for joinery, you should establish an identification system for your work so

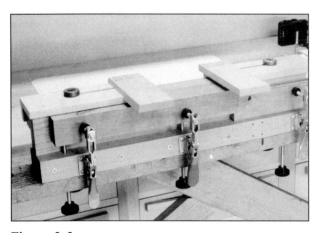

Figure 2-3
The workpiece here in my mortiser is indexed by the stop at the right and the templates above.

that you always know top from bottom, rear from front and the various face sides of all the parts. Sometimes I use inked-on arrows on the end grain to indicate face sides and handedness (Figure 2-5). *Handedness* refers to whether a workpiece, is left- or right-handed in its assembly. Incidentally, if like pieces, such as legs, are symmetric—equal in all respects—they are *unhanded*. I'm not timid when it comes to marking the face, and I have no qualms about marking up the face of the board with a no. 2 pencil. I'd say one-third of my early work errors were from crummy identification practices.

Using Stops

Stops are adjustable edges and surfaces that limit the travel of a workpiece or machine. They can also help position a workpiece for a repeatable operation such as cutting equal lengths on the radial saw. Stops are aids to the indexing procedure. Most machine work, like drilling, sawing and routing, requires stops for safety, accuracy and repeatability.

CHOOSING MEASURING AND LAYOUT TOOLS

The joinery process involves two measuring steps: the layout process and the fit itself. Sometimes pre-layout measurements are necessary for the layout (a drawer or door opening, for example). The pre-layout and layout tools are generally the same tools.

A lot of woodworking measuring tools are

STOPS

Stops can be as simple as a block clamped to the face of the router-table fence (Figure 2-6). The overhanging template and the fence act as stops in positioning the work in this jig (Figure 2-7). In a third example (see Figure 2-4), a rabbeted stop is hooked on the end of the work so the template can be located in the same place from workpiece to workpiece.

Figure 2-6
This stop on the left of the router table fence limits the travel of the work and consequently the length of the open mortise I'm cutting.

Figure 2-7
A stop, besides limiting the travel of the work or its fixture, can position and ready the stock for a cut. In this example the fence and the template do exactly that.

offshoots from the carpentry and construction trades. While these tools are satisfactory for average work, precision tools will make joinery more accurate and predictable. Joinery is an exacting science that takes some patience, but it can be very easy and a lot of fun. Good joinery is your expression of excellence in woodworking.

L.S. Starrett, Brown and Sharpe, Mitutoyo and Bridge City Tool are the industry leaders in quality layout and measuring tools. As you gain experience and increase your skill level, the need for expensive layout tools diminishes. With experience, your habits shift from measuring everything to the more efficient cut-and-fit mentality.

Buy quality measuring tools: They are a good investment. Furthermore, if you take good care of them they'll last your lifetime, and you can depend on them. That simply can't be said for rafter squares, tape measures and plastic calipers. Layout and measuring tools will also prove essential and invaluable in calibrating and in making such things as templates, fixtures and jigs, which all play an important role in joinery.

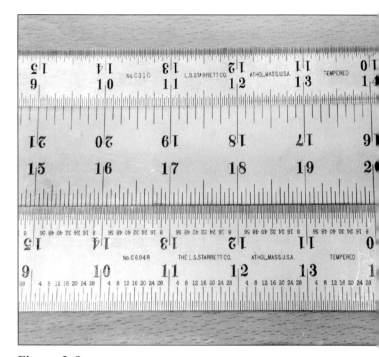

Figure 2-8
These satin chrome-finished scales can be read in the worst of lighting conditions.

The Rule

A 3′ satin chrome finish (nonreflective) C604R-36 Starrett rule covers a lot of layout and other measuring chores. The C604R-12, a 12″ rule, is ideal for shorter lengths and very handy for measuring the projection of a saw blade or router bit. The satin finish on these tools reduces the reflection so much that you can read them in any light. The layout tolerance for tools of this grade is such that your measurements will all read the same whether you use a 6″, 12″, 24″ or 36″ rule. You just can't expect this same performance from folding rules, tape measures or rafter squares. If you can afford it, 1′, 2′, and 3′ rules will meet most of your demands, and the 4′ model is a nice luxury if you make three- to

four-foot modules such as kitchen cabinets. These rules have six scales: halves, quarters, eighths, sixteenths, thirty-seconds and sixty-fourths. The halves, quarters, eighths and sixteenths are on one side, and the thirty-seconds and sixty-fourths are on the other (Figure 2-8).

The Hardened-Steel Machinist's Square

Precision squares are essential for close work. They get so much work and they're so important that I've accumulated several of them. I use one for machine setup, such as the table-saw blade, sander and jointer. Although these tools all have stops or gauges, I still use my 4″ Starrett to verify the setting. Small 1″ and 2″ squares are better at checking joint squareness—using more blade than necessary can confound your interpretation (Figure 2-9). I use the tool with the longer

Figure 2-9
My 4″ square is just right for checking the squareness of this joint. The 6″ Bridge City is also a try square but it can be used to scribe lines just as well.

blade (Bridge City Tool) for scribing and preparing material for cutoff: I like the feel of wood on wood for this job. To verify inside and outside corners and surfaces, I like the 6″ Starrett. The steel handle and beam make a distinctive scraping sound on 90° wood surfaces that helps me confirm squareness. The blade also "rings out" if it clunks just right onto a board at exactly 90°. The 6″ is also great for template-making operations and small jig and fixture setup. I have a 12″ luxury model for squaring up the larger jigs and checking panels for squareness.

There are many grades of squares, but the ones you can count on are hardened, ground and often supplied with certification. You need at least one good square, and either the Bridge City Tool 102-001 or the Starrett 20-6 can be considered industry standards in the wood- and metalworking fields, respectively. Both have about 6″ of inside-beam reach. If you are going to make joinery a lifetime pursuit, you should buy a few more squares as your budget allows. It's nice to have a backup or two, as they do wear out, and if one should hit the concrete, it

MAKING A STRAIGHTEDGE

If you don't want to buy a straightedge, you can make one that works surprisingly well from some hardwood sticks.

1. Select two 4′ to 6′ long × 4″-5″ wide × roughly 1″ thick pieces of very straight-grained hardwood such as oak, beech or walnut.
2. Joint their faces and plane to approximately ⅞″ thick.
3. Now joint one edge of each board, leaving the other edge rough.
4. Compare the jointed edges in a well-lit room or outside in the sun.

5. Turn one of the boards over end for end and compare again.

If a 2- or 3-mil (.002″ or .003″) feeler gauge will not slip between the sticks (held together only with hand pressure) over their full length in either orientation, either stick can be used as an acceptable straightedge. Keep in mind, though, that wood is constantly changing shape, and your two sticks may be straight today but crooked tomorrow. You'll need to check the straightness of your truing sticks before each use. Steel doesn't have this problem.

can only be used for rough work thereafter. Store these tools in wooden casework. They deserve a lot of respect.

The Straightedge

Straightedges come in many grades. For rough work, shear-cut tools are acceptable. (Rafter squares and rules are usually shear cut.) For close work, ground tool steel is the standard. The straightedge is not particularly a necessity for joinery; it is, however, critical for some setup procedures, checking the flatness of machine surfaces (e.g., jointer beds and table-saw tops) and verifying that you really are flattening your stock on the jointer.

If the edges of your stock are not straight, you will have trouble sawing, indexing, joining and doing the layout. A short straightedge like the 2' Bridge City Tool 101-003 is quite useful to check for machine-surface flatness and to set up jigs and fixtures. A 3' or longer straightedge is required for checking the flatness or straightness of jointed boards.

The Dial Caliper

The fit of a tenon in its mortise is dependent on its parallelism. "Fitness" is related directly to the consistency of the thickness of your stock. The thickness tolerance for good joinery is on the order of ±.002″. You cannot measure this difference without a precision measuring tool. Although you can feel a 2- or 3-mil (.002″–.003″) discrepancy between two adjacent boards, you can't tell whether the discrepancy is 2, 3, 4 or 5 mils. A dial caliper or its counterpart, the micrometer, is designed to measure thickness accurately. The thickness of the male portions of joints (tenons, tongues and dovetails) is just as important as the thickness of the female section,

and you need a way of measuring each.

The dial caliper is the best tool to measure inside, outside and depth. Starting out in machine joinery can be confusing, especially if you're used to ordinary length-measuring tools such as the folding rule or tape measure. In time, the need for a caliper diminishes, but early on you won't be able to pin down the sources of error in fitting without one. A plastic caliper, in my estimation, is not precise enough. Calipers that sell for about $35 are acceptable, but their quality is so variable I'm hesitant to purchase one. Good calipers, such as the Starrett 1207-6 or the 505 series Mitutoyo, run in the neighborhood of $75 to $125 and are considered excellent in the metalworking trades. A cheaper alternative is the micrometer, but generally they're sold in increments of only 1″, and unless you can buy a set of them they're not as useful as the dial caliper. Keep your eye out for machine shops going out of business or retiring machinists selling off their tools—you may save on the cost of a new tool.

Calipers should be kept in their cases when not in use; the gear racks are vulnerable to airborne chips and dust. A drop on the floor, whether tile, concrete or wood, renders the tool good for only rough work. Calipers are also

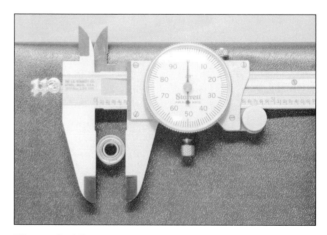

Figure 2-10
This R-3 bearing measures .500″ on my caliper.

great for measuring tool bits like router bits and drills. Keep in mind, though, that measuring carbide will shave away some of the jaw on these calipers over time and ruin them.

Even though calipers are really simple to read and use, there is a "touch" and a technique for using them correctly. Don't squeeze the jaws closed—they'll bend and give you false readings. Practice measuring on ball bearings: They're extremely accurate and they're made to tolerances tighter than a caliper can measure to. Practice measuring widths and diameters until you're able to get the same numbers over and over again (Figure 2-10).

NICE BUT NONESSENTIAL MEASURING TOOLS

Telescoping Gauges
Some years back I discovered that a dial caliper can read differently on inside and outside dimensions, depending on the wear of the respective edge of the jaw. That is, if an inside measurement is made on a standard gauge block and the dial is then adjusted for any error, the dial may

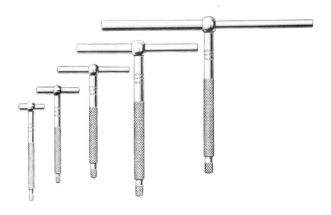

Figure 2-11
Telescoping gauges can be a little tricky to use but they're a nice luxury for inside measurements (photo supplied by L.S. Starrett).

not be calibrated to read the same error on an outside dimension. The error is usually only .0005″ to .0015″, but it can be worse if the insides of the jaws have been used more often. In joinery we're always measuring the inside and outside dimensions, so this can develop into a problem. If you know the error and always account for it, it's really not a big problem—but it is an annoyance.

The telescoping gauge solves the problem (Figure 2-11). Telescoping gauges are expressly designed to fit inside small openings. A Starrett 5229FZ set will cover the range of ½″ to 2⅛″. The measurement is a transfer technique: You fit and lock the tool in an opening and then measure the telescopic projection of the gauge with the inside of the jaw on the caliper. Not only is this a more precise measurement but, by using only the inside of the caliper jaw, the tool is always calibrated. The gauge is also handy when making various templates for slots, mortises or whatever. It's a luxury, but it's very helpful in tracking down minor errors that might otherwise slip by unchallenged.

The Universal Bevel Protractor
Two sticks can be cut and positioned in such a way that the tool that cut them can be shown to be adjusted very close to 90° without the use of a machinist's square. The procedure used is nowhere near as handy as using a 90° square, but it can be done quite well without any tool.

Angled measurements or settings on woodworking tools are not like those on metalworking machine tools. Sometimes, on very expensive woodworking machines, the gauges and fences are very good, but they still don't approach the accuracy and precision of metalworking tools.

Nevertheless, if you have a universal bevel protractor, not only can you verify any bevel

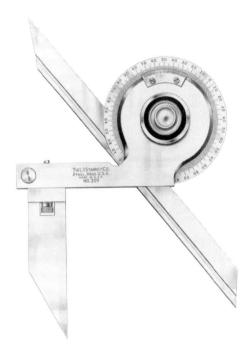

Figure 2-12

A bevel protractor can simplify setup, and you can track errors on beveled work with confidence. It is an expensive tool, but if you work with strange angles on a regular basis you might consider one (photo supplied by L.S. Starrett).

angle on the workpiece, the tool also will verify the right angle (90°). A measurement on the work might show that a change in the miter gauge or fence angle has to be made. The precise amount of angle change is really a "by guess and by golly" on all the equipment I'm used to. I usually just cut and fit, and then guess at the new setting and start out all over again. With a bevel protractor, you can set and calibrate the angle before the cut. You can verify the work and transfer the angle settings to another tool. A bevel protractor can make up for the poor dial, fence or other angle indicators found on most woodworking tools. Admittedly it's a great luxury (Figure 2-12), but in this phase of my woodworking life I'm getting lazy, and I'd like to apply more of my skills to product design and quality than to fiddling with tool adjustment.

Good bevel protractors cost between $80 and $250, depending on their features, adjustability, origin and so on.

The Marking Gauge

The hand joiner usually marks out, scribes or otherwise draws his joinery boundaries on the work; the machine joiner may also do so. It may seem strange to you, but I almost never mark out the joints I cut. I pay particular attention to the orientation, position and workpiece identifications, but I don't mark out or otherwise lay out joints. I have a marking gauge, but I only use it on plywood and veneers to score cross-grain fibers so they won't tear out from the router bit. If you work to the scribe line, you might save some time if you try my approach. I will describe the process as we cut the joints, but briefly here is how I work.

I always cut spare material on each mill run for all the parts to be joined. The spare stock is exactly the same size as the "project" stock and is used for the machine setup. I usually estimate the geometry of the joint and cut sample joints on the scrap. I make the necessary judgments, and then I use the remainder of the scrap for refinements and for the final settings of the jigs, fixtures and other tooling. I may mark a rough line here or there to aid in the setup, but the line is merely an aid—not a true cut line. The cuttings are measured often and verified to be correct by the "fit," not by cutting to a scribe line.

CUTTING AND FITTING JOINTS

In the final analysis, the elements of a joint must fit together nicely. Not only is the fit important for the adhesive to work well, but if the joint is on display, part of you is too. Furthermore, the integrity and usefulness of your project depends on a good fit. A good fit for gluing is different than the fit for sliding joints, knock-down joints or other connections that are not to be glued. The joints in this book are considered to be glued joints.

Joints for gluing should be "slip fits." The sloppiness for a joint of this sort should be around 1 to 3 mils (.001″–.003″): More slop can be tolerated, but not less. A tolerance of this sort is not difficult to achieve with routing techniques (I'll prove this to you later on). For now let's concentrate on the fit itself. The qualities I'm asking you to recognize are simple to detect. It's the slip fit. If the assembly needs to be hammered together, it's too tight. You'll squeegee the glue right off the work if a hammer is required. If the joint rattles, knocks or can be twisted a few degrees, it's too loose. Some joints will glue up in this condition, but don't expect a lot of service out of a loose fit. Putting the work together is like extracting a playing card from the deck or replacing a card into a handheld fan of them. The surfaces all scrape one another, but there is not much resistance to the insertion. This condition is best achieved with a cut-and-fit approach.

A measure-and-fit approach is essential for those starting out, but eventually you'll find that cut, try and fit is the most practical way to cut router joints. One of the reasons for this is that measuring and calculating are sources of error that are simply not present in the cut-and-fit strategy.

Measure and Calculate Anyway?

It is quite possible you are more comfortable measuring and calculating—and sometimes it is unavoidable. Unfortunately, for most of us, the English system of dividing an inch all the way to

sixty-fourths is about as error-prone as it gets. Close work will require you to add odd and even quarters, eighths, sixteenths and so on. For example, can you add $^{17}\!/_{64}″$ to $2^{1}\!/_{32}″$ in a jiffy? A good door or drawer fit may depend on a calculation like this. Now, not only is there an opportunity to screw up the measurement, but with fractions like these you're far more likely to screw up the arithmetic.

What can you do about this? Buy a fractional calculator. A fractional calculator (the Construction Master IV, for example) adds fractions, and as long as you punch the right keys you'll avoid arithmetic errors: one less source of error. Fractional calculators have saved me a lot of time (Figure 2-13).

Figure 2-13
This calculator can operate on fractions. It will add or subtract odd fractions in any order and reduce them to the lowest common denominator (photo supplied by Calculated Industries).

SIMPLIFY THE CUTTING PROCEDURES

Just as the fractional calculator can simplify your computations, there are procedures in router joinery that markedly cut down on error. For example, the fewer number of cuts you make and the fewer number of setups, the fewer your mistakes. This conservation-of-energy strategy is Nature's own way—it should be yours as well.

Symmetry

A lot of cuts and joints in this book are symmetric; that is, the joint is the same on both sides of its center line, and it was made that way because equal amounts of material were removed from both sides of it. This tactic greatly simplifies and improves the accuracy of your joinery. It does, however, impose high standards on material preparation and jig making. There is always a tradeoff. There are few giveaways in wood joinery, but the more you know about it, the simpler it gets. (And, I might add, that last statement is not trite.)

When I first started out, the information I had at hand suggested that all I needed to join wood was a Sears ¼″ router and some scrap. My early work was awful, took forever and was not fun. Today, not only are most of the joints I make easy and fun, I usually do a pretty good job of it.

Simplify Cutting Setups

Most of the time there are two members to a joint: one essentially female and the other male. If the cutting process to make both members requires two or more machine setups each, the fit can, and most likely will, be quite variable.

There are many reasons for this, but mainly it's related to (1) the difficulty inherent in routers "finding" their correct depth of cut, (2) jigs and fixtures that are poorly cobbled together, and (3) stock that is badly milled.

If one member of a joint can be made at one depth with one machine setup, nearly all your joinery will be a snap. On outside cuts this means you do not change the fence setting (or edge guide), nor the cutter height, to make that sex of the joint (Figure 2-14). On inside cuts, that means one-cutter-diameter cuts at one depth (Figure 2-15). The final depth is reached with the router set and locked once, and the guide is never moved to widen an excavation.

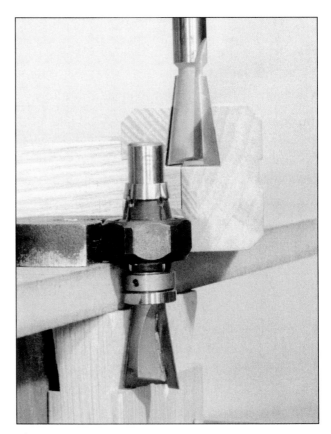

Figure 2-14

Both sides of the dovetail tenon (an outside cut, below template) are cut at one depth of cut and one fence setting. Do not cut the joint in stages unless you use two routers. The final pass must be done without any machine adjustment.

Figure 2-15
This sample set of dovetails was used for the setup on the legs and rails of my router table. The dovetail pins are one cutter diameter in width. The sockets are also one cutter diameter (see top of Figure 2-14).

There will, of course, be occasions where a router and its cutter can't plow to final depth in one pass. In those cases it is permissible to use another router with a smaller cutter to do most of the dirty work at various depths and fence settings. The final cut, however, *must* be done in one pass with a router preset to final depth, thus excavating a new and final path exactly the same size as the cutter.

Consistency Improves the Fit

Cutter rotation, feed direction, clamping forces and machine and jig (fixture) stress all play a part in how well your joints fit. For the most part their combined influence is constant from workpiece to workpiece and nothing to worry about. If you make a change midway through your joint-making run, however, look out! Feeding the work on the router table the opposite way, to save a fence setting perhaps, can not only be dangerous but also bends the cutter the opposite way, which can change the shape of the cut. Hand-feeding the router from left to right after ten runs right to left may loosen a clamp or impose a little new but opposite backlash that can widen a cut. There are a lot of these quirks in router woodworking, but if you're consistent they may never be a problem. As marvelous as they are, routers can't do everything well. Know their limitations!

LIMITATIONS OF HAND ROUTING

I really like hand routing, and for more than ten years I did all my routing with a portable tool. I feel like I have more control, and when the cut is a hand cut the results are usually better. Nevertheless, and quite fortunately I might add, whenever the hand router is deficient, the router table fills in splendidly.

MESSY JOBS

Routing is messy, dusty and noisy, but fun, accurate and precise. Mess, dust and noise can be minimized on the router table. Doors and paneling can be added to the table for noise abatement. An exhaust funnel should be installed in the fence to collect the chips and dust. And managing the power cord and a stack of unwieldy workpieces is simply easier on the router table. If a table job can be done just as well or nearly as well as by hand, I'll use the table just for those reasons. The benefits are worth any sacrifices.

ROUTER TABLE LIMITS

Some router-table cuts are simply too dangerous or impractical. For example, climb cuttings—stock fed left to right when facing the cutter (cutting with the rotation of the cutter)—can rocket the work right out of your hands. In all honesty, I do occasionally climb cut on the table and it's always at some risk. If the stock removed is equivalent to less than ³⁄₁₆″ square, the cutter is sharp and the work is easy to handle, I'll climb cut. You must realize I have twenty-five years of experience and I know the outcomes and hazards of all the climb cuts I do. Climb cuts markedly decrease tearout—and there's my one and only incentive to do it. Work done with sharp cutters and light cuts while feeding stock right to left (anticlimb) can also be tearout-free. Try a lot of anticlimb cuts before giving in to the climb cut: It's a dangerous and unpredictable practice. Be especially cautious widening slots and such (more than one cutter width), as you may unwittingly climb cut while feeding right to left.

JOINING LARGE AND SMALL PIECES

Work of all sizes is subject to being joined. And there will be occasions, when working on the router table, when a joint done on one workpiece will be safe, while the same cut on another, much smaller or larger piece is a hazard. These conditions should be obvious, but they may not be. If you are in doubt, try the cut on scrap first—or at the very least, run through the procedure with the cutter retracted just to see if you can manage the stock safely.

The joinery processes in this book are not accidental. They are derived from a long history of experimentation, trial and error. The choice of whether to table rout or hand rout has been made for you. The safest and most accurate way to join is always the way I've chosen. You may not like it—the jigging may be more than you want to tackle, and you may be satisfied with your present method. I don't know it all and quite often my students outsmart me, but rest assured the cuttings I do are fast, accurate, consistent and safe—and the parts fit together.

The Bearing or the Fence?

While we're still on the subject of router tables, let me make one last plea. A good router table is flat with a straight fence that is square to the table. Anything less can cause problems with the fit and the control of the work. Most joinery is straight-line work, and therefore the straight, square table/fence system should be exploited as much as possible. A bearing-guided cutter is a marvelous invention, but for straight-line work on the table, it is redundant and can actually produce joints of lesser quality than those created just using the fence. One reason for this is that the bearing bounces over every defect, while the fence can't feel any of them.

I don't normally use bearings on the table, although there are times when I have no choice. One such case that comes to mind is the cope-and-stick joint for door rails and stiles. These cutters are generally stacked on one arbor and spaced by a bearing. The bearing here is simply a requirement of the cutter/arbor assembly. In every case where a cutter is assembled on its arbor, as opposed to a solid cutter assembly (Figure 2-16), and a bearing is included as part of that assembly and its function, it should not be tampered with. A solid rabbet bit that is supplied with a bearing, on the other hand, should have its bearing removed during straight-line work on

Figure 2-16
This cope-and-stick cutter assembly is spaced correctly on the arbor by the thickness of its sandwiched bearing. Don't tamper with it. This rabbet bit is not an assembly and works well on the router table without the bearing.

the router table. If ever you're in doubt, leave the bearing on but adjust the fence so the bearing is just out of play.

The Collar Guide or the Bearing-Guided Cutter?

A collar guide is usually a two-piece ring-and-nut assembly that is fastened to the router subbase (Figure 2-17). The device surrounds the cutter and is slid along and held against a template so the cutter can excavate a pathway. The pathway can be any shape, including a square hole such as a mortise. The engineering requirements for a collar to be exactly centered to the cutter are enormous. Most collar-guide systems are

CLIMB CUTTING

Climb cutting is a hazardous practice because the work can be unexpectedly pulled from your hands. It is also dangerous and difficult to do because a uniform hand feed is often interrupted as the cutter is steering the work away from the fence. This competition between the operator and the router produces an uneven cut that will, in some cases, require a second or third pass. Since the first cut is uneven, the second will be as well. The feed is often abrupt, jerky and uncertain. All the while the cutter engagement and rotation are such that the work is being pulled out of your hands in the direction of feed. To overcome these uncertainties requires a lot of practice and the understanding that some work simply cannot be cut safely in the direction of cutter rotation—no matter what.

While I do not advocate climb cutting, I take these precautions when I do climb cut:

1. Use new or near-new sharp cutters. (Climb cutting is not nearly as efficient as anticlimb; sharp cutters make it easier.)

2. As the board is struggling to accelerate out of my hands, sometimes I use rubber gloves to hold on to the work.

3. I never climb cut work less than 12″ long or 3″ wide. Anything smaller puts my hands too close to the cutter.

4. I may rout 70 to 80 percent of the cut in anticlimb so only 20 or 30 percent of the cut is climb. Shallow, light cuts are safer. The bigger the cut, the more the cutter is engaged and the more apt it is to throw the work.

5. Never rout an unwieldy stick. If you can't feed the board safely right to left, you'll never safely climb cut it.

Note: If you frequently fall back on climb cutting as your silver bullet, you should consider a power feeder.

UNPILOTED BITS

Bearing cutters can be used on the router table, but I usually don't do this. If I'm straight-line routing, the fence, not a bearing, is my guide. Bearings are useful and sometimes mandatory for curved work, but most table work is done on the straight sides of a workpiece up against the fence. There are a couple of reasons I rarely use piloted bits on the router table. The first is economic. Unpiloted bits, especially straight cutters, are cheaper than analogous bearing-guided rabbet bits—and I don't have to replace a bearing on a cutter that doesn't have one. The second reason I don't use bearings on the router table is that edge defects transfer. If you are using a pilot bearing against a less-than-perfect edge, every defect will transfer to the profile. Moreover, it's usually the case that the frequency of the edge joint defects are such that they cause minor resonances ("bearing bounce"). These vibrations usually work-harden the edge and produce a chattered profile (Figure 2-16A). Frequently these defects can be sanded out, but they don't occur when a fence has been

Figure 2-16A
The sample on the bottom was cut off the fence while the one on top was cut using a bearing. The edge defects on the sample cut off the fence did not transfer to the profile.

used. A straight, square fence can more than average out the edge defects. And if the workpiece and fence are really straight, the cuttings are better than the edges they're produced from—a real plus. If you must use a bearing-guided bit on straight work, adjust the fence so that the bearing is out of play.

rarely centered to the cutter, but they're close enough for most work.

In joinery, if you can work off the same quadrant of the collar (and not rotate it around as you work), it matters little if the cutter is centered or not (Figure 2-18). However, using collars to cut joints for handed work, such as the left and right legs of a table, can be confounded by this collar/cutter eccentricity. If your cuttings are the same but shift slightly from workpiece to workpiece, it might be due to this anomaly. Use collars only in situations where precision isn't important. Two-stage cuts where the first part of

the cut is cut with a collar system and finished with a bearing-guided cutter is one approach. The laps we'll cut are done this way (see chapter eight).

Bearing and cutter manufacture are very exacting processes. Pattern cutters (Figure 2-19) with bearings on the shank are so accurate that their errors are way beyond anything that would affect the fit of the joint. The accuracy of your joinery is calculable and predictable with bearing-guided cutters. Beware, however: "Nothin's perfect." Errors do occur on occasion, and you can expect a little variation in the work if the

Figure 2-17

A Porter Cable offset subbase (shown unattached to its casting) with Porter Cable's collar guide assembly is an excellent ensemble for safe and controlled collar template cuts.

Figure 2-18

Routing while the offset knob is parallel to the template's edge is the most practical way to rout with an offset base. For clarity, a wide scribe line is painted on the template. Keeping the knob on the line keeps the same section of the collar against the template, so any cutter/collar eccentricity is going to be the same from workpiece to workpiece. Consistency is an important component of precision in routing.

Figure 2-19

This is an array of some of the pattern cutters I use. Always match the flute length of the cutter to the thickness of stock as closely as possible.

cutter has been sharpened a time or two.

Joints can be cut in more than one way. There are more than ten million woodworkers in the United States. With that much diversity, you can count on a lot of variation of themes. Joinery is no exception. I know people who are quite satisfied with the most unorthodox methods; others are looking for the better way, and still others haven't done enough to know the best way.

If you can accept that, you should be able to accept defeat if a particular cutting sequence is consistently bad or variable. If your routed joints are troubling you, try another method. An adjustable and lockable edge guide like the Microfence is a lot more trouble-free than sliding a stop or tapping it with a hammer. A bearing-guided cut is more accurate than a collar-guided one, and a table-cut centered tongue is usually better than one cut off a rabbet bit using the pilot bearing. There are also plenty of times when one sex of the joint should be table-cut and the other should be hand-cut. Be flexible and plan on a smorgasbord of techniques for best results.

THE EFFECT OF CUTTER QUALITY ON THE JOINT

A fresh, sharp cutter is likely to give the best results, given good wood and fixturing. Bad cuttings and excessive tear-out are often the result of dull or worn cutters. How long has it been since that cutter was sharpened? Carbide bits are indeed hard, and you wouldn't expect them to wear out in an afternoon, but they can. Cutting 300′ of hardwood under medium conditions is often considered the limit for most carbide router bits. A 10′- to 20′-per-minute continuous feed rate on a cutter can wipe it out in less than an hour! You can't expect perfect results from worn cutters. They burn the stock, they require excessive feed forces and they cause tear-out.

STRAIGHT-LINE WORK

Straight-line work is quite ordinary within the art of joinery. Glue jointing, tongues and grooves, open mortise work and jointing are all straight-line in nature. Although these processes can all be done with templates, edge guides and the portable router, they are best done on the router table. The support, steerage and mess control are all reasons for this efficiency on the table.

CUTTER LIFE

If you have a lousy cutter, you're really at a disadvantage. Here are some tips about cutters that will improve your joinery.

1. Use ½″-shanked tools whenever possible. They're stiffer, stronger, easier to regrind and last longer than ¼″ tools.

2. Be aware of uneven wear on a tool bit. If you've made 150 ½″-long dovetails on a 1″-long cutter and now decide to make longer ones, a wear line will show on the work at the ½″ level. If the wear is severe enough, the joints won't fit. That goes for the other joinery tools such as slotters, straight bits and rabbeters, too.

3. For maximum tool life and crisp joinery, use two cutters, one in each of two routers. Do the majority of the cutting (more than 70 percent if possible) with one tool and make the finish cut with a freshly ground bit or one with lower mileage.

4. Sharp cutters are the keys to cuts free of tear-out. If you're burning wood, using excessive feed forces or chattering the cut, you should suspect your cutter. Try a new cutter without changing anything else. If the new cutter in the same router cuts clean, you know the cutter is at fault.

5. For safety's sake, keep at least ¾″ of shank in the collet. If the cutter is excessively extended, it will chatter the work—and it could break. (*Chatter* is a result of excessive cutter vibration or the work vibrating against the cutter. This excessive vibration causes a hammered, "chattered" appearance on the work.) Cuttings produced from cutters that don't vibrate are nearly perfect.

6. A cut greater in area than the equivalent of ⅜″ square is often the threshold for excessive feed forces and other stress factors. Try and keep your cuts lighter than this. Big cutters in big routers are more tolerant of big bites. A ⅜″-square bite of wood should be considered the limit for a 1½ hp router.

Cabinet Door Stiles and Rails

Router-table work is size-sensitive. On my table all I can handle is about 25 pounds of stock. A 6/4 board 6' to 8' long and 5" to 7" wide is about 25 pounds. Stock smaller than this is much easier to handle—kitchen cabinet door stiles and rails, for example. They are often a little narrow, but they're far easier to table-rout than to hand-cut. The rail ends are cut across the grain with a fairly large and intimidating cutter to form the joint. This cross-grain cut, if done with a portable tool is dangerous and subject to error because there is so little support for the handheld router, and a lot of cutter is engaged in the work. The miter gauge or a similar sliding jig on the table is the safest way to rout these parts (Figure 2-20).

ROUTER-TABLE–SPECIFIC CUTS

There are plenty of borderline cuttings that can be hand-routed: open-ended mortises, sockets for loose tenons and long-grain dovetails. They are, however, dangerous and extremely cumber-some when done by hand and require very sophisticated jigging. Cuts like these are the natural province of the router table.

Edge-guide cuttings for joinery in general can also be table-routed better than by hand, though there are exceptions (Figure 2-21), such as mortises, large assemblies and when you have to see the cut. For example, in router-table work, the cutter is hidden; if you must see the cut in progress, edge-guide work is called for.

Joinery can be fun and rewarding, although, it does take some practice and an understanding of the principles. The greatest tooling in the world, however, will not make up for a lack of knowledge and experience. Don't get caught up in buying a lot of stuff for router joinery because you think it's going to make it easier and faster. A mind-set that says "Boy, if I only had this or that tool" is only trading one set of problems for another. Fancy routers and cutters can make the work easier, but it is quite possible to do all the joinery in this book with just two routers, a router table, five to ten cutters, a few simple handmade jigs and some clamps. Good luck and hang in there—you'll like it, believe me.

Figure 2-20
My miter gauge blade is sandwiched between two parallel pieces of MDF. This tactic keeps the blade parallel to the fence, simplifying adjustments.

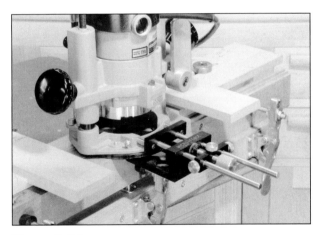

Figure 2-21
Working this mortise with Richard Wedler's Micro-fence edge guide is an excellent choice here. When a single-cutter-width mortise is called for, finding its center is really sweet with this fully adjustable tool.

CHAPTER THREE

Cutting Tongue-and-Groove Joints With a Router

TONGUE-AND-GROOVE JOINERY BENEFITS

In the production cabinet shop there is no time to make close-fitting tongues and grooves. In most cases the adjoining workpieces are just painted with glue, aligned and nail-gunned together. In furniture-grade situations one must make time—and for the consumer, there's an added premium to pay. There are many arguments for and against the use of tongues and grooves (T&Gs), but for the moment I'd like to concentrate on just one: They save time!

Time-Saving Joinery

Making fine furniture and cabinetry is a time-consuming proposition. It is also a process of constant time shifting: As you get better at it, you get faster. One way you get faster is by improving on processes up front that save you time later on. If you do a crummy job gluing up panels, for example, you will have to either do a lot of hand-planing and sanding or send it through the planer again. If you replane, you have the expense of lost time and the loss of more material, and you perhaps run the risk of more planer tear-out.

Efficient Joinery

If you join well-milled stock evenly using tongues and grooves, often only a hand-sanding is needed to ready your panels for the next operation. As a rule, the work required to make tongues and grooves is more than made up for in efficiencies as your project proceeds.

TONGUE-AND-GROOVE BASICS

There are many possible joining schemes with tongues and grooves. I'd like to address three of them. In this chapter we'll join boards edge to edge (long grain), as in a panel glue-up. We'll also join long-grain tongues to face-grain slots (long grain), as in making L-shaped legs, and finally we'll form simple short tongues for cross-grain slots in applications such as shelves in dados or drawer backs joined to drawer sides (Figures 3-1A, B and C).

Tongue-and-Groove Tooling

There are a lot of cutters, including dedicated tongue-and-groove sets, that can produce tongues and slots (Figure 3-2). Some of the cuts we'll make are done more safely and accurately,

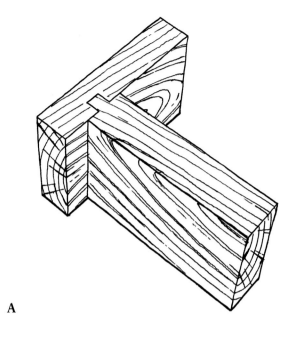

A

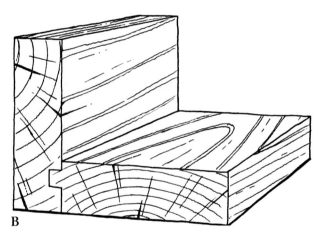

B

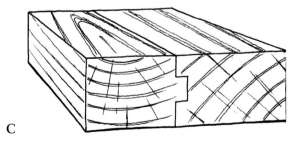

C

Figures 3-1A, B and C

Drawings show the following assemblies:

A. End to face cross-grain (drawer backs to sides)

B. Edge to face (both long-grain)

C. Edge to edge (for panels, etc.)

Figure 3-2

Here's an ensemble of carbide-tipped tools that are capable of cutting the tongue, the groove or both. The Amana wedge and tongue set (center) is an example of a dedicated system. It works best in material from ¾" to 1³⁄₁₆" thick.

and more expeditiously, with a hand router and jigs, while other cuts will be table-routed. The routers, cutters, jigs and processes I've chosen are not simply random choices. All of the techniques and gear shown (and used) here are the best methods I know to produce the best results as safely as possible in the least amount of time. I have also chosen what I think are the best cutters, not only for their value but for the range of work they can handle. I use tongues and grooves more than any other joinery process, and this chapter concentrates over twenty years of my experience with this type of joint.

Joint Mechanics

Tongues and grooves are indispensable in my woodworking because of the way they mechanically interlock and register one board to another. They provide an interlock not found in a butt joint, and they provide additional surface area for glue. The assembly process is facilitated with T&Gs, and the joint is stronger, in many instances, than dowels, biscuits or nails. Joints that are tongued and grooved also last longer than similar joints without tongues and grooves because they tolerate far more impact and seasonal dimensional stresses. Furthermore, there is more latitude with glue application than with a butt or biscuit joint because of increased surface area (typically 25 to 65 percent more). And finally, it can be argued, they look nice.

EDGE-TO-EDGE LONG-GRAIN TONGUES AND GROOVES

Edge-to-edge long-grain joints are essentially used to create panels. In this instance I am referring to wood, though the same rules apply whether you're joining plywood to wood, MDF (medium density fiberboard) to itself or other common materials to one another. The router table is used for both cuts here.

Material Preparation

I'm assuming you've read chapter two carefully, and that dimensional control and squareness are under your command. Aside from straightening, flattening and thicknessing your stock, you could ignore a parallel rip at this stage if you'd like. I usually joint both edges of the boards I tongue-and-groove and save the rip for the glued-up panel. Interestingly, it is often the case that the panels I make are parallel to within ¼", even though I usually don't ripsaw any of the individual boards that make up the panel.

I believe a well-sawn surface is acceptable for tongues and grooves, but stress relief during the rip often contorts a board just enough to make it handle funny on the router table. For example, if any crook has been introduced, the depths of both the slot and the shoulder of the

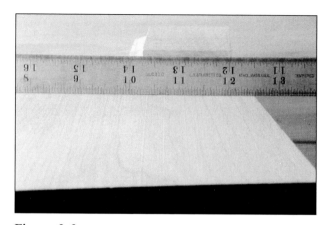

Figure 3-3
Even though the knife blades on my jointer are solid carbide, they wear and chip just like high-speed steel. The relatively uneven cut on the face of this freshly jointed board, while acceptable for presentation to the planer, is unacceptable for edge gluing.

tongue will vary. I made a dedicated router/jointer table to edge-joint all my stock. With its carbide bit, I can joint plywood or even MDF if I have to. A cast-iron jointer is just as good, but the knife wear on the jointer is usually so variable that my edges sometimes aren't as good as I'd like them to be (Figure 3-3). With my router/jointer, if the cutter is dinged or worn in increments I can change it in two minutes. If I change the knife blades in my jointer, I'm out an hour—easily. I made the right investment with my router/jointer, but it was a substantial one in terms of time, design and materials. (For more on router edge jointing, see my book *Getting the Very Best From Your Router.*)

The Cutters and the Cutting Procedure

Either sex of the joint can be cut first. The joint is cut on the router table. The tongues are cut with rabbet or straight bits, and the slots are cut with three-wing slotters. The tongues are

FOUR KEYS TO SUCCESSFUL EDGE-TO-EDGE JOINTS

1. Let the thickness of the tongue be about one-third the thickness of the work and as shallow as possible (Figure 3-4). Boards of nearly any thickness can be joined edge to edge: They needn't be the same width or thickness. Tonguing the thinnest boards (saving the groove for the thicker sticks) saves time and material. The widths of the tongues I make vary between an ⅛″ and ³⁄₁₆″ (Figure 3-5).

2. Allow defects (cosmetics or torn grain, for example) up to the width of the tongue on those boards that will be tongued. If the tongue is ³⁄₁₆″ wide then any defect up to ³⁄₁₆″ will be erased during the tongue-cutting operation (on either side). A defect of this width would have to be ripped off if the boards were butt-joined. In the event of such a defect (while making the T&G), you will have saved the rip, wasted the defect and produced a tongue all in one step.

3. Keep the narrow boards as wide as possible. Random-board-width assembly is more economical than equal-board-width assembly. In random-width assembly there will, of course, be some narrow boards. A very narrow board is usually out of place—unless, perhaps, it's in the center. In any event, try to keep those marginal, narrow-width boards to a maximum width by not tonguing them: Slot them instead. (Two tongues ³⁄₁₆″ wide on the same board will effectively narrow its face by ⅜″.)

4. Wavy-grain boards get the slots. Routing long grain can be essentially free of tear-out if the grain is straight and the cutter is sharp. In those cases where the grain changes near the edges, tear-out can and will occur if the cut is anticlimb (against the cutter rotation). Boards with wavy or wild grain changes near the edges should be slotted so if tear-out occurs, at least it'll be hidden in the groove.

Figure 3-4
A normal edge-to-edge T&G.

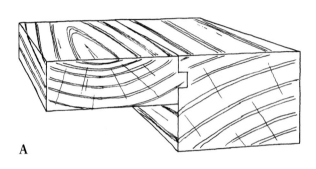

A

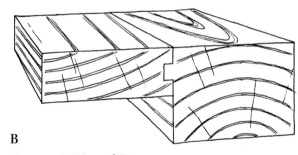

B

Figures 3-5A and B
It should be clear from these drawings that tonguing the thicker piece is more time- and energy-demanding than tonguing the thinner piece. Therefore it makes more sense to slot the thicker of the two.

centered by virtue of symmetry: An equal amount of material is removed from each side of the stock. The slots are centered in the same way: The work is fed to the cutter face-side up and face-side down without changing the depth of cut. (Curiously, equal amounts of material are not usually cut away while slotting, but the cuts are centered nonetheless.)

Cutters for the Tongue

The tongue is a rabbet cut on both faces of the stock; as such, a rabbet bit is the best bit to use. A Jesada Tools 835-850 is an excellent choice for rabbets less than ½″ square. Straight cutters also work well. Almost any straight bit will work, but the most effective cutters have flutes from about ½″ to ¾″ in length and cutting diameters from ⅝″ to about 1″; all have ½″ shanks. A Jesada 801-690 (¾″ cutting diameter [CD] with ¾″ flute length [FL]) or an RS4-48 (from Paso Robles Carbide [CD = ¾″, FL = 1″] are both good starting points, but there are literally hundreds of choices from many sources.

Keep in mind that a flute length much longer (20 to 30 percent) than the vertical depth of the rabbet is unnecessary and just invites cutter deflection. The radius of the cutter should be more than the sideways depth of cut, starting at about ⁵⁄₁₆″ (minimum cutter diameter is therefore ⅝″). I would not use a ½″ cutting diameter bit, as there is too much grinding into the shank, weakening it, and therefore too much cutter deflection.

Cutters for the Slot

The slotted member of the joint should be cut with a slotter, with the work flat on the table. Do not attempt to cut slots with narrow, straight bits with the work on edge. Slotters from Jesada, PRC and Grizzly cover just about all the slotting I've ever encountered: Three-wing slotters are excellent, but two- and four- wing slotters are also acceptable.

Slotters are usually used for T-molding and other commercial applications. They were not intentionally designed for the groove of a tongue-and-groove joint, but they might as well have been. They're perfect for the cut: They zing right through wood just like a saw blade. Cutters from the three suppliers mentioned previously vary in thickness from ¹⁄₁₆″ to ½″. If you keep the tongue/groove thickness to about one-third of the stock thickness, these cutters will work on stock as thin as ³⁄₁₆″ or as thick as 3″ without a change in depth of cut!

Slotters are similar to saw blades in that they cut and are relieved for cuts on the top, bottom and ends of their teeth. Be aware that some rabbeting bits also cut this way and are therefore candidates for the cut as well. If you are in doubt, use only those cutters that are specified as slotters.

Use the Router Table

The router table is the best way to cut tongues and grooves. If you use slotters and rabbeters, the boards to be tongued or grooved are fed to the cutters flat on the table, not on edge. For consistent and precise cuttings, your fence, as well as the tabletop, must be flat, straight and inflexible. If any one of these three requirements is not met, your results will be inconsistent. Tabletops with plastic inserts with routers attached can deflect. If you use a router-table system with plastic inserts, you should consider using a stiffened ⅝″- or ¾″-thick slab of MDF with a router bolted directly to it instead (Figure 3-6).

Cutting the Long-Grain Edge-to-Edge T&G

The wood I buy is rarely the width I need for panels, desk tops or even drawer fronts. Even if

Figure 3-6

The relatively thin (⅝″) MDF surface is kept flat because it is bolted to six 2¾″ × 1⅜″ beams. You may not agree with the practicality of my table design but it works well, and if I have fitting problems it's not related to any contortion in the work surface.

it is, I usually rip it, joint it, plane it and glue it back together to relieve any stress in it that may haunt me later on. If your stock is milled flat and of equal thickness with square, straight edges, you have half the equation met for good tongues and grooves. This joint is done on the router table, so if your router table is flat, if its fence is straight and if you decide to follow my instructions, you can cut perfect tongues and grooves before the day has ended.

It makes no difference whether you cut the tongues or grooves first. For experience, cut them both ways, since there will be occasions when you may have to start with either a groove or a tongue. A ³⁄₁₆″ side-to-side (lateral) depth of cut is typical, so let's start by making a tongue ³⁄₁₆″ wide, one-third the thickness of the stock. Let's use 1″-thick material.

STEP 1 Select a rabbet bit or a ⅝″-diameter or larger straight bit. Collet up the tool.

STEP 2 Set the vertical depth of cut. It is not critical, but keep it as close to one-third the thickness as is practical (²¹⁄₆₄″ to ¹¹⁄₃₂″).

STEP 3 Adjust the fence to take about ³⁄₁₆″ of stock. Again, this depth of cut is not critical.

STEP 4 Now rabbet all the boards requiring tongues on both faces (Figure 3-7), producing centered tongues. The tongues should be around .333″, or a nominal ¹¹⁄₃₂″ thick by ³⁄₁₆″ wide.

STEP 5 Select a slotter that is thinner than the tongue but whose thickness, doubled, is greater than that of the tongue. This ensures that the vertical depth needn't be changed to produce the correct slot. A ³⁄₁₆″ slotter will do. Remember: One machine setting for either or both sexes of the joint will simplify the process enormously.

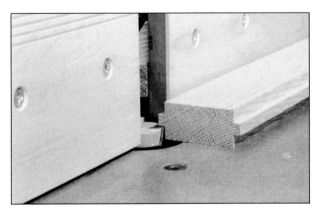

Figure 3-7

The fence is set to allow about ³⁄₁₆″ depth of cut. The cutter height is about one-third the height of the workpiece. Dividing the work into two passes like this (one rabbet per side) is easier on the cutter, and the cuts are usually pretty clean and free of tear-out as my sample is here. Note the absence of an end-bearing.

Figure 3-8

Set a tooth of the slotter to a depth that is parallel to the bottom of the tongue.

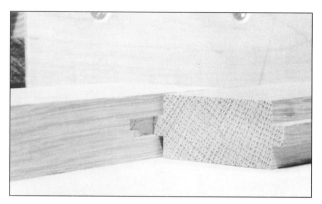

Figure 3-9

Obviously the tongue has a long way to go before its shoulders reach the edge of the slotted workpiece. The fit in thickness is correct, however. I've slotted only a few inches of the "calibration" stick.

Figures 3-10A and B

(Top) The depth of cut is correct now. All the surfaces meet up smartly.

(Bottom) My fence is of the pivot design and now I want to change its position by about the thickness of a dollar bill (.004"). Two thicknesses of a dollar at the lead screw will change the position at the cutter (the midline of the fence) one thickness.

STEP 6   Collet up the cutter and set the fence to cut less than the tongue width. Adjust the height of the cutter so that the bottom of a cutter tooth is parallel with the bottom of the tongue cut in step 3 (Figure 3-8).

STEP 7   Cut a slot on the edge of equal-thickness scrap material; turn the board over, changing nothing; and repeat the cut (Figure 3-9). Check for a slip fit. Adjust the cutter up or down until a slip fit is achieved.

STEP 8   On the same piece of scrap, continue slotting (both faces) while changing the fence setting until the shoulders of the tongue just "kiss" the edge of the slotted piece of scrap (Figures 3-10A and B). Once that condition is met, increase the fence setting so the slot width is deepened by about the thickness of a dollar bill and slot all your stock, passing the cutter with the face side up and the face side down. This completes the joint.

EDGE-TO-FACE-GRAIN TONGUES AND GROOVES

Edge-to-face-grain (long grain) assembly is more common than you may think. The garden variety "face frame" cabinet is a perfect example, and this joint also occurs a lot in jigs and fixtures, and in furniture applications such as L-shaped table legs (Figure 3-11).

This cut, in my view, should also be a table cut. The cuts are negotiated easily enough, but as a rule the tongue is offset from the center line, and therefore two machine settings are required for it. The slot should be cut in one pass at one depth. It should also be noted that generally the slotted member cannot be flipped over for the symmetric cut, so, by necessity, the slot is a single-depth, single-cutter-width cut.

On occasion the T&G assembly may be so far from the edge of the slotted member that a slotter cannot access the site, and therefore a straight bit will be called on for the slot. A long-grain slot, cut with a straight bit while the work is flat on the table, is quite acceptable; slots cut with straight bits on the edge of stock are unac-ceptable to this woodworker for safety and quality reasons.

The easiest sequence of cuts requires the tongues (offset) to be cut first, followed by the slot. Two shoulders are more advantageous for assembly and for hiding any tear-out or sloppiness in the slot, although one shoulder is often acceptable. The offset tongue should be positioned to leave at least ⅛" on the short side.

Cutting Edge-to-Face-Grain Tongues and Grooves

STEP 1 Collet up either a straight or rabbet bit and set its height for ⅛" or more. Cut one side of the tongues with all the common faces of the stock face down on the table. The fence setting for this cut is arbitrary, but somewhat dependent on the thickness of the piece to be slotted. (I would set the fence to cut a tongue one-third or less as long as the thickness of the slotted workpiece).

STEP 2 Cut the other side of the tongue to fit a sample (one cutter width) slot of the

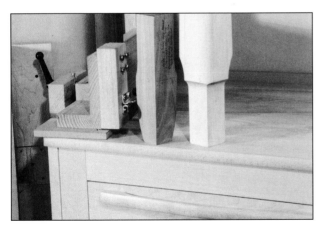

Figure 3-11

These table leg samples and the jig demonstrate a face-grain to long-grain slot. The front face of this beechwood cabinet also sports an edge-grain to face-grain T&G where the frame meets the side panel.

Figure 3-12

Check the thickness of the tongue in a slot sample that was cut with the actual cutter you intend to use for the slots.

Figure 3-13A
Some slots will be out of reach of your arbor. Paso Robles Carbide, however, makes an arbor (foreground) long enough to reach about 2¼" safely from the edge of the stock on my router table.

Figure 3-13B
The completed joint.

intended slotter. The tongue is usually one-third the thickness of the tongued stick, although this too is arbitrary, since all of the glue line is long grain (Figure 3-12).

STEP 3   Select and collet up the appropriate slotter. Now, on scrap, take a single swipe, with the grain, on the edge or face. Verify that this new slot fits all your tongues. Adjust the fence until the slot is as deep as your tongues are long, plus the thickness of a dollar bill. (These are all calibration cuts.)

STEP 4   Now raise or lower the cutter to suit, and slot all the work with the appropriate face pressed against the fence (Figures 3-13A and B).

WOOD GLUES

Wood glues, to me, are just as miraculous as wonder drugs are to health. Ordinary adhesives are virtually blind to long grain, edge grain, cross grain, zigzag grain or any cut for that matter. Wood glues to wood (Figure 3-15). If the joint is cut well, if the glue is applied adequately and if the clamping forces don't move anything out of square, even an end-grain to face-grain connection is astoundingly strong.

Figure 3-15
Look at all the torn grain from the face of this sample; it was end-grain-glued to the block shown. I used ordinary yellow glue (Borden Carpenters' Wood Glue). It took a pipe clamp (used as a lever) to break the pieces apart. There were no dowels or any other joint; it was simply butt-joined.

CROSS-GRAIN SLOT TO END-GRAIN TONGUE

This tongue-and-groove configuration (Figures 3-14A, B and C) is not as popular as the other two examples, but it is important. It is also usually done on the table saw, but I'm convinced it can be done much better with routers. The typical application of this joint is seen in the assembly of drawer backs to drawer sides, shelves to dados and, on occasion, cabinet sides to tops. Every facet of the joint joins long grain to end grain (in lumber), but I can assure you, if the joint fits well, it will glue up well and provide a very serviceable connection. A screw or reinforcing dowel here and there will offer additional pull-apart resistance if desired.

Cutting the Cross-Grain Slot to End-Grain Tongue

The joint is best cut with a jig and hand router (the jig is described on page 61). Both pieces should be cut with the work fixtured vertically. Each sex of the joint can also be cut on the router table, but the work is difficult to handle and even a slight cupping of the work will yield results that are variable or done at some risk. In the jig, the work is indexed and pressed flat so those handling problems (on the table) are absent. The jig is simple and is used with a template and collar guide or bearing-guided cutter. The router of choice is of the fixed-base design; for control, use an accessory offset subbase (see the List of Suppliers on page 139).

The tongue should be cut first, and any offset required of its center line should be accounted for as in the previous example. Since the tongue is likely to be offset and therefore require two machine setups, the groove should be made in one pass at one cutter width. This tactic

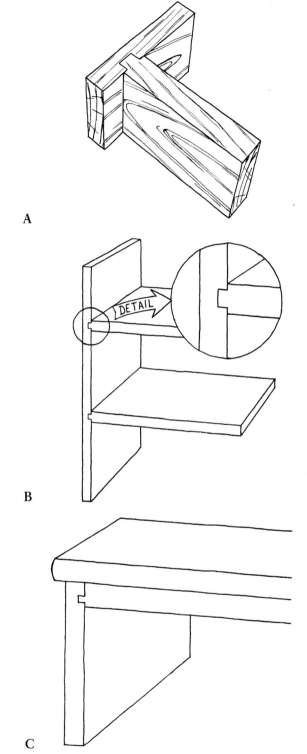

A

B

C

Figures 3-14A, B and C
Drawings of cross-grain slot to end-grain tongues.
A. Drawer back
B. Shelf dado
C. Cabinet subtop into sides

always simplifies the process. (If the tongue is centered, the process is further simplified.) The tongue can be cut with nearly any short, straight bit, but the RS4-48 (½″ shank, ¾″ cutting diameter × 1″ flute) from PRC and the Jesada 801-690 are two excellent choices. These cutters cut equally well on the bottom or sides of their flutes. To guide the cutter path, use a Porter Cable 42021 template guide (inside diameter = 1¹/₃₂″). Grind or hacksaw the length from its supplied ⁷/₁₆″ to about ⁵/₁₆″. The net length isn't critical, but make sure it's shorter than the thickness of your template (Figures 3-16A and B).

If the tongue is shorter than ½″, a common occurrence, use a PRC TA-170 (see Figure 3-19, page 56). As a shank-bearing–guided cutter, the TA-170 requires no collar guide and therefore can be worked directly off the template. There are many TA-170 equivalents, but the PRC is a more reliable cutter choice since its cutting diameter is always a few thousandths of an inch less in diameter than its bearing, and therefore it won't cut the template. If a cutter purposely or accidentally cuts a template, it and the template are useless: Many of these trimmer type cutters I've tried have cutting diameters larger than their bearings and will destroy a template.

Figure 3-16A
I hacksawed and then sanded the end of this Porter Cable 42021 collar guide down to about ¹¹/₃₂″. The cutter is a PRC RS4-48 which is an excellent choice, though most short straight cutters will also cut well.

Figure 3-16B
The extension of the collar is less than the thickness of the template. A stub-tenon cut is shown in progress.

CUTTING THE TONGUE FOR A CROSS-GRAIN SLOT AND STUB TENON

STEP 1 Index the work on end and clamp it in place against a ⅜″- or ½″-thick MDF template (Figure 3-17).

STEP 2 Position the template (for offset tenons/tongues) to cut about a ⅛″ shoulder.

I'm using ¾″-thick stock here: If your stock is thicker or thinner, adjust the shoulder accordingly (Figure 3-18).

STEP 3 Rout this shoulder of the tongue on all the common pieces on their common faces. Small cuts of this sort, on end and of this volume, can be climb cut and, as a consequence, there's essentially no tear-out. This unfinished cut

Figure 3-17
Gently hold the work against the fence and up against the template and clamp it in place.

Figure 3-18
My template has a nifty toggle clamp on it (under the cleat). Adjust the template to cut a ⅛″ cut.

shows the direction of the cut (climb cut) and just how little tear-out there is (Figure 3-19).

STEP 4 Now reload the work with the uncut face facing out. Clamp in place and re-position the template to cut the other shoulder. (**Note:** If the tongue is centered, no change of the template position is required.) The resultant tongue should be of such a width (thickness) that it fits a sample single-slice/single-cutter-width slotter cut (Figure 3-20). This cut should be repeated on scrap until you achieve a tight, albeit a slip fit in your sample-slot cut.

STEP 5 Now cut all the stock to create either centered or offset tongues (short tongues on the end of stock are also known as *stub-tenons*).

Cutter Selection for the Cross-Grain Slot

For slots from zero to 3/16" deep, use the appropriate-width bearing-guided groover from PRC. Their cutter-width choices are 1/8", 3/16", 1/4", 5/16", 3/8", 1/2", 5/8" and 3/4" (Figure 3-21). If the desired cut is less than 3/16" deep, use a Porter Cable 42021 collar guide (shortened to 5/16") and a 3/8"- or 1/2"-thick MDF template to regulate the depth. Omit the collar to achieve a 3/16" depth.

If the required depth is more than 3/16", many of the off-the-shelf slotter/bearing combinations will be acceptable (e.g., Grizzly rabbet series C1040–C1558). The above-named cutters, bearings and arbors cover a lot of slot possibilities and will work from zero to about 2" from the end of stock. If the depth and location of your slot are out of this range, a straight cutter, template and/or edge guide can be used.

Figure 3-19
Rout this 1/8" shoulder on the common face of all your stock. I'm using a PRC TA-170, so I don't need a collar guide. The bearing works right off the template.

Figure 3-20
The second shoulder is now being cut. You might want to cut this one oversized on scrap, repeating until the cut fits nicely in a sample of the slot produced by the slotter you intend to use.

Figure 3-21
This PRC family of groovers will cut a groove up to 3/16" deep in widths from 1/8" to 3/4" in one pass.

Cutting the Slot With Work on End

STEP 1 Collet up the appropriate cutter/collar to cut a single cross-grain slot. Adjust the cutter extension (vertical position) so the slot occurs where you want it. Adjust the template if one is called for.

STEP 2 Index a piece of scrap and clamp it in the jig. Now cut the work in a single pass. If correct, cut all those pieces requiring the slot (Figures 3-22A and B).

Cutting the Slot With Work Flat

STEP 1 Select the appropriate straight cutter that is the same diameter as the thickness of the stub-tenon. Use a fixed-base router and offset subbase, such as a Porter Cable 690 and Porter Cable 42193 subbase. A 1" O.D. (outside diameter) collar is also required (Porter Cable 42030). Adjust the extension of the cutter to equal the length of stub-tenon plus the thickness of the template (in step 2) plus a dollar bill.

STEP 2 Make a right-angle template 3/8" or 1/2" thick (see page 58), locate it and clamp it on the work (Figure 3-23). The

Figure 3-22A
Here, I'm making the cross cut with a PRC groover. They make a 4"-long arbor so it's possible to cut at least 2½" from the end of the stock. Get some experience first, however, before extending the cutter that far. (My thumb is on the subbase, not the cutter!)

Figure 3-22B
The assembled joint.

Figure 3-23
One of the nicest ways to make a cross-grain slot (dado) is with this setup. Clamp the template in place and use a router with a collar guide held snug against its edge for a straight-line trip across the work. A Porter Cable 690 and their collar-acceptable offset subbase (41293) are the perfect team to keep the router flat smack down and the collar pulled against the guide.

MAKING AND USING THE RIGHT-ANGLE TEMPLATE

There's nothing special about my template. It's simply a slightly modified Old English bench hook. Make several to accommodate the various widths of the boards you rout. I have one with 6″ of work edge for small stock, a 12″ model for shallow cabinets and an 18″ one for larger casework. Make the template from ⅜″- or ½″-thick MDF at least 7½″ wide. Position and fasten a cleat under the template so the work edge is at a 90° angle to it. The work edge must be free of defects, since a bearing or collar guide will copy any deviation onto your work. A toggle clamp will facilitate the use of the template (Figure 3-24).

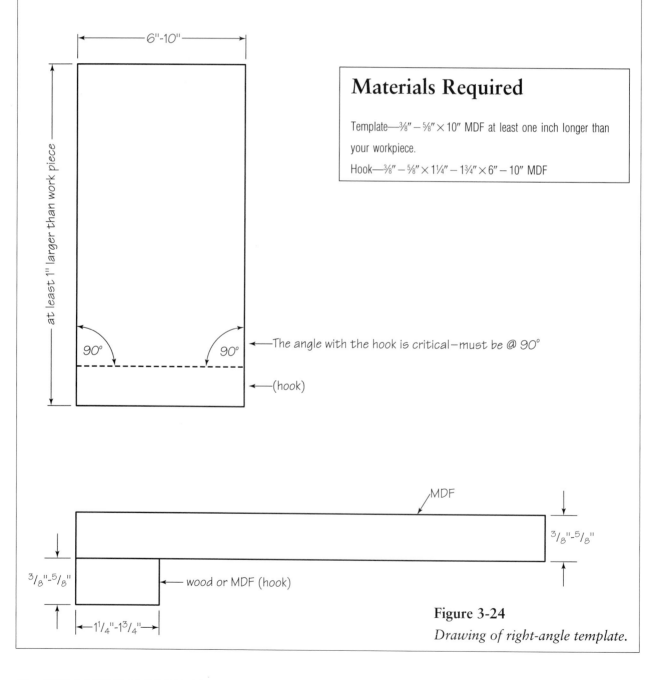

Materials Required

Template—⅜″ – ⅝″ × 10″ MDF at least one inch longer than your workpiece.

Hook—⅜″ – ⅝″ × 1¼″ – 1¾″ × 6″ – 10″ MDF

6″-10″

at least 1″ larger than work piece

90°   90°   ←The angle with the hook is critical—must be @ 90°

←(hook)

MDF

³/₈″-⁵/₈″

³/₈″-⁵/₈″   ← wood or MDF (hook)

1¼″-1¾″

Figure 3-24

Drawing of right-angle template.

correct location of the template is found by adding the intended center line location of the cutter (measure from the end of the board) to one-half the diameter of the collar, in this case ½″. For example, if the cutter center line is to be at 5″ from the end of stock, measure 5½″ to the template and clamp it in place.

STEP 3 Cut the slot while pulling the offset knob inboard, thus snugging the collar against the template. A cut from left to right will keep the collar against the template with more purchase than if the cut were made from right to left. Any deviation from a straight line down the guide will spoil the cut, so keep the collar against the template.

CONSTRUCTING A ROUTER BEAM JIG

A 34″ × 6½″ beam, although quite short and narrow, can easily support a 50″-long × 10″-wide board, since only 8″ would be hanging off each end and 1¾″ off each side. If you make your beam like mine, you will be pleasantly surprised at just how easy ordinary routing can be; you will also find that the end of the jig makes difficult end cuts such as making tenons a snap.

This beam is only 6″ high, so you'll need to rest and clamp it to an existing surface. I use mine atop the router table, which is heavy enough to be stable. The combined height puts the surface at 42″. I mounted a Jorgensen 175 deep-throat design C-clamp on it. I had a pre-drilled ¼″-thick × 1″-wide × 4″-long steel plate welded to the fixed end so I could screw it permanently in place (Figure 3-25). Just where the best place is to locate it on the beam is uncer-

Figure 3-25
I had the fixed end of this Jorgensen 175 C-clamp welded to a predrilled ¼″-thick piece of steel. I screwed the clamp to the underside of the beam so it only takes one hand to operate it.

tain; you'll have to experiment.

To make the beam you'll need about 7′ of 6½″ wide 5/4 material. I used red oak, but I would have used beech, maple, birch or ash, in that order, if I had had the stock on hand. Select the straightest boards for the best resistance to distortion. Mill the board or boards to 1″ ± ¹⁄₁₆″. This simple but unbraced structure is rigid at 1″—it may not be at a lesser thickness. The knock-down joinery is simply shallow tongues and grooves reinforced with steel cross dowels and bolts (Figure 3-26). I chose knock-down assembly for strength, and I can always take it apart for repairs. Moreover, if I need to add a fixture or jig, I can work the individual elements.

I designed my jig with an 8″ overhang to facilitate clamping (Figure 3-27). The other 2′ of the underside of the beam is clear of all clamp

Figure 3-26
I routed some shallow tongues and grooves to register the parts of the beam. Then I drilled through the joints for joint-connector bolts as shown here. The beam is not glued, so I can always take it apart to repair it or add stuff on.

obstacles so a workpiece can be clamped anywhere on either side of the jig. The work surface also has a through keyhole slot (Figure 3-28) in it so a router, even with its cutter extended, can rest flat (subbase down) over the hole. The keyhole is camouflage to hide an accident I had when I accidentally started a router in the hole. A 1½″ hole is all that is necessary.

I put a stick on the edge of the end piece, which is flush to the inside and situated 1¾″ below the work surface (Figure 3-29). The stick measures 1″ × 1¾″ × 17″ and is square to the

Figure 3-28
I routed this keyhole slot to waste away a splintered-up mess I made when I accidentally started a router. A 1½″ or 2″ hole in the beam will allow you to rest your router with an extended cutter flat on its subbase.

Figure 3-29
I bolted this maple fence to the edge of the end piece. It serves to register any workpiece, like the one shown here, square to the top of the jig.

MAKING AND USING THE JIG FOR ON-END CUTS

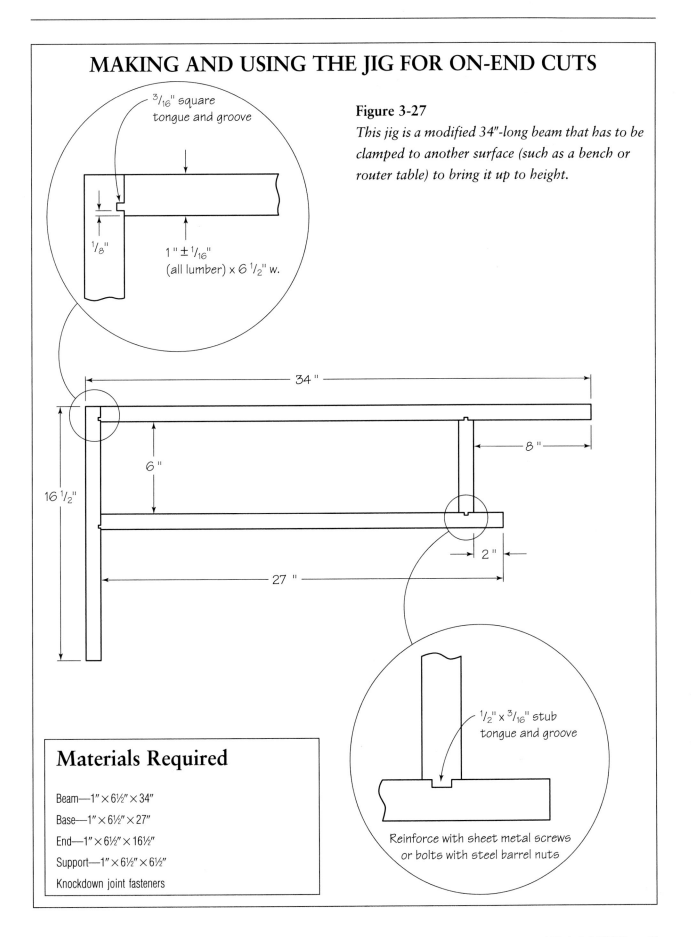

Figure 3-27
This jig is a modified 34"-long beam that has to be clamped to another surface (such as a bench or router table) to bring it up to height.

$^3/_{16}$" square tongue and groove

$^1/_8$"

1 " ± $^1/_{16}$"
(all lumber) × 6 $^1/_2$" w.

34 "

8 "

6 "

16 $^1/_2$"

27 "

2 "

$^1/_2$" × $^3/_{16}$" stub tongue and groove

Reinforce with sheet metal screws or bolts with steel barrel nuts

Materials Required

Beam—1″ × 6½″ × 34″
Base—1″ × 6½″ × 27″
End—1″ × 6½″ × 16½″
Support—1″ × 6½″ × 6½″
Knockdown joint fasteners

Figure 3-30
Check the fence-to-surface squareness. If you cut the end panel square, and if the beam that goes into it is 90° to the outside face of the panel, the fence will be square to the work surface. If it isn't, try to shim it square or just mount the fence on the face rather than the edge which is easier to square.

work surface (Figure 3-30). It functions as a stop and as a reference for stock indexed vertically. Using a 90° template, template collars and assorted bits, I can make sliding dovetails, two-faced tenons, slots or decorative end cuts on stock to 6½″ wide (Figures 3-31, 3-32 and 3-33). If end cuts are important to you, make the width of the jig consistent with the width of the boards you intend to rout. You can omit any joinery and just use cleats and no. 12 or 14 flat-head sheet metal screws. If you screw into end grain, use screws at least 3″ long.

Figure 3-31
You can take big bites off a workpiece on end like this. Nevertheless, get some practice taking ⅜″- to ⅝″-long cuts before trying a big dovetail.

Figure 3-32
The second cut on this tenon produces a two-faced centered tenon. Your workpiece has to be well dimensioned for a reversal cut because each of its edges is referenced separately off the fence.

Figure 3-33
Experiment—sooner or later you can use what you've learned in a folly. Here I'm using a subbase guide to control the lateral depth of cut on a series of stripes cut at different but even steps.

CHAPTER FOUR
Designing and Routing Tenons

TENON BASICS

The mortise-and-tenon joint is no accident. The joint is centuries old, and there are many variations. It can be very strong in its own right, but its effectiveness is often the result of a combination of just how well the joint has been routed, whether it has any reinforcement (such as a wedge or connector bolt) and just how it is tied up in the structure it resides in.

If you look at the joint in this way you can more easily deal with its design and your own limitations. For example, if you can only make short tenons, you might consider some easy way to apply some hardware to increase the joint's strength (Figure 4-1). If the joint is in a cabinet whose carcass entraps the assembly with tenons and mortises (a drawer blade, perhaps), why overkill with through tenons and wedges? And, finally, if the joint has little help from its family members in its assembly for strength (a gate, a door), more attention should be paid to a quality fit or some type of reinforcement. The point is, the criteria for the best mortises and tenons

Figure 4-1
This shallow tenon would easily pull apart without some reinforcement. There are two joint connector bolts in the assembly that make it indestructible. A loose joint connector bolt and barrel nut are shown for your understanding.

needn't be followed to the letter, as there are sensible alternatives for any compromises.

Applying Routers to Tenon Making

A router was not invented to cut tenons or mortises. Band saws, table saws, jointers and radial saws are helpful in wasting and some tenon-making procedures, but they weren't specifically designed to cut tenons or mortises either. The backsaw and the Japanese dozuki do nice tenoning, but equal measures of patience, skill and practice are required just for openers. Chisel-and-chain mortisers were expressly designed for mortises and double- and single-end tenoners (strictly production tools) likewise are job specific. These last two tools, largely unavailable to the hobbyist and the small shop, also require you to be rich, to be involved in large-scale production and to have an in-house setup man. The router has its limitations too, but with a few jigs and some cheap cutters, remarkable mortises and near-perfect tenons are possible. In my view there is no other single electric tool with this economy and capability. It is an excellent alternative: The skill required isn't demanding and it is the shortest route (no pun intended), both in time and practice, to achieving mortise-and-tenon (M&T) capabilities. Furthermore, if the jigging is sophisticated enough, light to medium production is possible, as the cutting times are often under 30 seconds for each procedure.

THE FIRST GRADE OF TENONS

By first grade, I mean the simplest tenons with the least amount of jigging. I'm also talking about two-faced tenons cut with the work held flat and horizontal. There are a lot of applications for two-faced tenons, but since they lack a third or fourth shoulder, they can't be used at the extremes (the ends) of legs or stiles unless the mortise is open-ended. Two-faced tenons are therefore more commonly found in reinforcing rails, in midline situations or in carcass work (Figure 4-2).

BUILDING THE TENONING TEMPLATE

There are at least two ways to rout the tenon: My approach is with the hand router. It can be

Figure 4-2

The tenon in my trestle bench is two-faced. I also reinforced it with two through dowels right through the leg.

TENON DESIGN

Tenons can be unfaced, single, two-faced, three-faced or four-faced (Figure 4-3). There are as many faces to a tenon as there are shoulders. An unfaced tenon has no shoulders: It's merely a stick cut to length. All the shoulders can be equal (a centered tenon) or be different.

Shoulders offer resistance to twist and rack and a means of hiding any error in the fit. They may also make an M&T possible, as a tenoned rail can, on occasion, be larger in section than the leg or stile it enters! As a rule, centered tenons are the easiest to make.

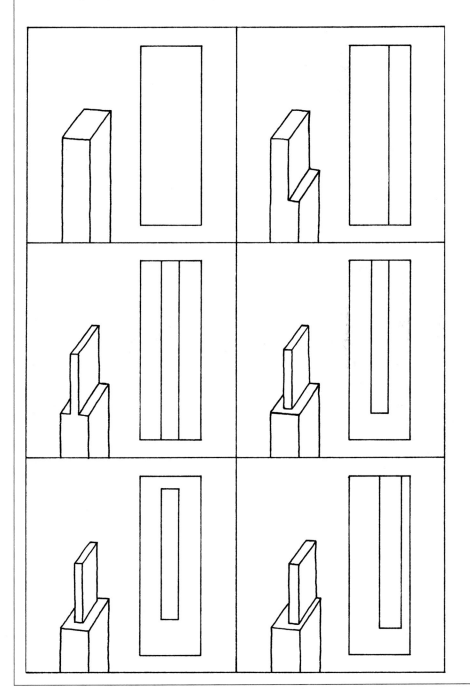

Figure 4-3
From left to right and top to bottom, these tenons are in order of increasing complexity. The end grain is shown next to each sample.

done on the router table, but in my view, tenons routed by hand are always superior to those done on the table—and it's safer. Along with a hand router (a Porter Cable 690 or a DeWalt 610 fixed-based router with an offset subbase, for example), a template and, at times, a template collar guide are required. As a router woodworker, this stuff should already be in your inventory, but the specialized template will have to be fabricated.

This template is designed for material of any thickness, widths to 2¾″ and any length. The depth of cut is limited to about ½″ or more, depending on the cutter you use, and the maximum length of tenons cut with this template design is restricted to about 2″. Study the design,

Figure 4-4
Two-faced tenon maker. The x and y dimensions (3½″ and 2″ respectively) can be adjusted for bigger or smaller stock. Add 1″ to the x dimension for every ½″ of stock width you'd like to tenon over 2¾″. Add, inch for inch, to the y dimension for tenons over 2″ long.

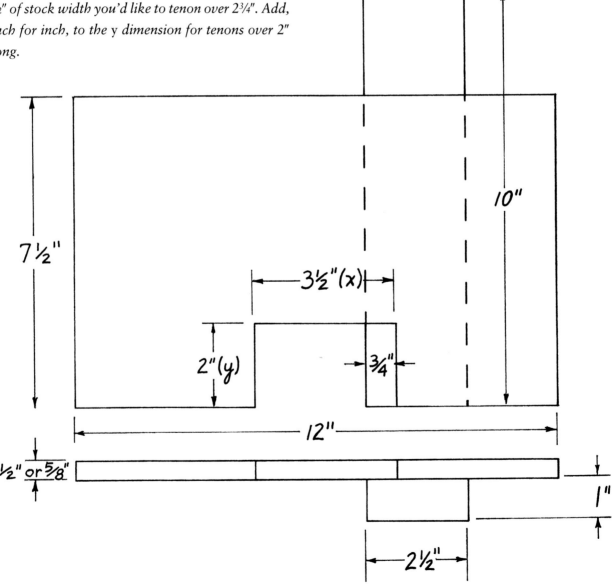

and if the template is underdesigned for your needs, make the changes now (Figure 4-4).

1. Select a piece of ½″- or ⅝″-thick MDF and cut it to 7½″ × 12″.

2. Rout, band saw or jigsaw a 3½″ × 2″ notch from one of the long edges, starting 3″ from the top. Add at least 1″ to the 3½″ dimension for every ½″ of stock width you wish to tenon over 2¾″. Add equivalent length to the 2″ dimension for tenons longer than 2″. The edge of the 3½″ dimension must be straight and free of defects, as this edge is the only edge of the notch that a cutter bearing or collar will slide against. A straight guide, a straight bit and a collar may make the best edge for you (Figure 4-5).

3. Cut a piece of hardwood 10″ long, 2½″ wide and 1″ thick. Add accordingly to this last dimension for work you intend to tenon over an 1½″ in thickness. For example, if you intend to tenon stock 2″ thick, increase the thickness of the piece (the reference fence) to 1½″.

4. Locate and screw the reference fence ¾″ below the top of the notch with its end flush to the working edge of the template. Its long reference edge must be exactly 90° to the working edge of the template (Figure 4-6). Any deviation here produces a shoulder on your tenons that is as deviant to 90° as your reference fence is to the working edge of the notch. Fasten with at least four no. 12 flathead sheet metal screws, with the heads on the MDF side of the template. The shank of the screw should penetrate the reference stick as deeply as possible.

5. Now, if you'd like, mount two 225-U De-Sta-Co clamps on 4″ centers so you can clamp the work to the template. If you don't want to spend the $20 for the clamps, just C-clamp your work to the template. You are now ready to rout one- or two-faced tenons accurately.

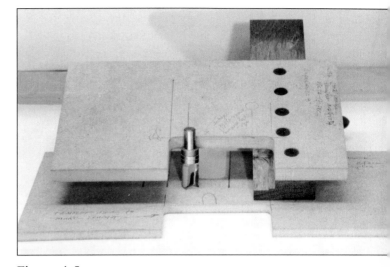

Figure 4-5

I made a template (under jig) to facilitate cutting the notch in the jig. I used a pattern bit to trim the notch accurately. You needn't be so exact. A straightedge located ¹⁄₆₄″ or so beyond the edge (if band-sawn) and a flush-trim bit for the cut are all you need. It's OK to bump into the top and bottom of the notch with the cutter, as those edges are never used for making tenons.

Figure 4-6

The angle of the reference fence to the working edge of the notch must be 90°.

ROUTING THE TENON

1. Position the work against the reference fence and extend the end of the work beyond the working edge of the template equal to the length of tenon desired (Figure 4-7) and clamp in place.

2. Use a PRC TA-170 for depths of cut to ½″ and a Jesada 811-127B for depths from ⅜″ to ¾″. Set the cutter to the final depth, as it is possible that multi-depth cuts will spoil the neatness of the shoulder. A fixed-base router should be used here because of its superior stability (Figures 4-8 and 4-9).

3. For cuts deeper than ¼″, consider using a collar guide and straight bit to waste at least 80 percent of the cut. Set the final depth of cut to ⁷⁄₁₆″ using the TA-170 and waste the remaining face of the tenon (Figure 4-10).

4. Turn the work over and repeat the cut for a two-faced tenon (Figure 4-11).

5. A third or fourth shoulder cut is possible by indexing the work on edge. It is likely, however, that the toggle clamps will be out of range and a C-clamp will be needed to hold the work (Figure 4-12).

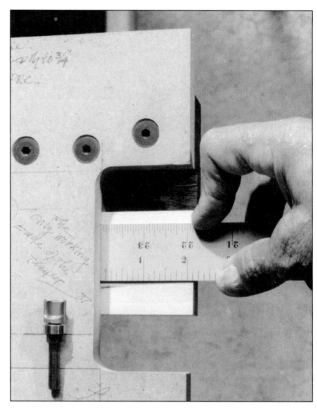

Figure 4-7

I can measure directly from the template to the end of the work for the correct tenon length. You might notice I used some big machine screws to fasten the template to the fence. If you stagger your screw pattern with no. 10 or no. 12 wood screws you'll have a structure just as strong.

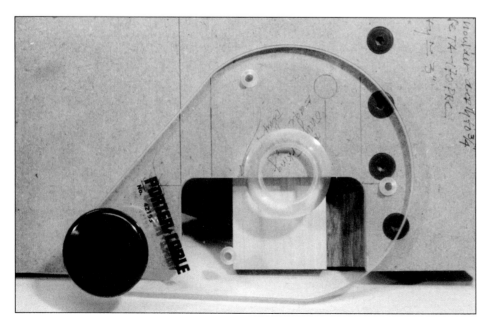

Figure 4-8

A Porter Cable 690 offset subbase (see the List of Suppliers on page 139) or a larger base of some sort are necessities to rout this joint. The window through which you are routing is just too big for a standard base casting to span safely.

Figure 4-9

Before routing the interior of the cheek, trim at least ⅛" from the perimeter as shown. This tactic, along with holding the work against the fence, will prevent any tear-out.

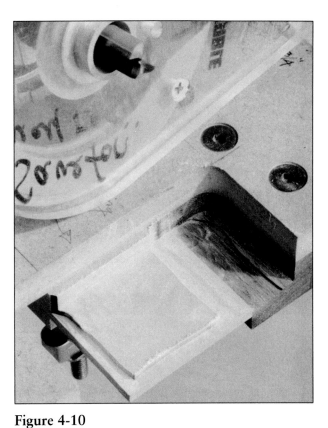

Figure 4-10

The final depth of cut is ⁷⁄₁₆". I've taken the cheek down to ⅜" using a Jesada ⅝" diameter straight bit and a Porter Cable 42030 collar. I've started the final pass with the flush cutter (PRC TA-170). The shoulder cut is a full ³⁄₁₆" × ⁷⁄₁₆" but the rest of the field is only a ¹⁄₁₆" × ½" cut, a modest cut indeed.

Figure 4-11

The completed two-faced tenon. I'm always amazed at just how well this TA-170 bottom-cuts in spite of its very spartan flute design.

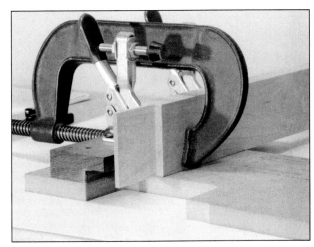

Figure 4-12

A third or fourth shoulder cut is possible in the jig if the work is positioned as shown.

WORKING ON END

Cutting the tenons while the workpiece is held flat has certain advantages, among which are the simplicity of the jig, the ability to cut very long tenons, no tear-out, the use of a cheap cutter and safety. The cutter does about the same amount of work on its end as it does on the side of its flutes, and the shoulder is produced from the side of the flute, where the cuttings are far more efficient.

Working the tenons on end positions the cutter to the work in such a way as to present the cheek of the tenon to the side of the flute and the shoulder to the cutter's end, just the opposite of the conditions of cutting while the work is flat. I make this observation for a couple of reasons: One is that in spite of these grand differences in cutting, position and jigging, the character of these routings is nearly indistinguishable! Router bits are really awesome and, indeed, engineering masterpieces.

The second reason I mention the distinction is to illustrate a limitation. A flat template system can be made to accommodate very long tenons—4″ to 5″ is within the practical range. On-end cuttings, on the other hand, are limited to the length of motor travel of the router (up and down) and the shank and flute lengths of the tool bit. This translates to a tenon length of about 2½″ or less.

TWO-FACED TENONS CUT WITH THE JIG FOR ON-END CUTS

The cuttings for these on-end (two-faced) tenons are produced from the jig for on-end cuts in chapter three. The procedure is the same as that for stub-tenons. A template, straight bit, collar and fixed-base router are required. The only area of concern is in handling the router. I strongly recommend a medium weight (2 hp) fixed-base tool with an offset subbase. The offset subbase will aid in holding the router flat, and the offset grip knob will help you pull the collar against the template. The cuts in the flat-template approach are rarely over ½″ deep and the cutter sweep is only a ½″-wide path. There are few control problems there. Cutting on end is a different story: A 2″-long tenon requires 2″ of cutter extension—a rather dangerous proposition.

In order for you to gain confidence with this type of cutting, cut a lot (dozens) of tenon cheeks ³⁄₁₆″ by less than ¾″ long before attempting to cut long ones (1¼″–2″). (Long tenons can, of course, be cut safely with repeated shallow cuts.) The danger is that if you accidentally tilt the router, the cutter may suddenly be cutting too much into uncharted territory and grab and perhaps kick back (Figures 4-13A and B show a radical case of tilted tool). If you have any reservations about cutting with a lot of cutter extension, you should consider the flat-template approach.

Selecting the Cutter

I have selected a cutter from the Whiteside Machine Co. inventory that will cut a 2″ cheek, the 1087. It's a deflection-free tool, solid carbide, spiral-ground, with a down-shear and good bottom-cutting capability. This is an excellent tool, although there are literally hundreds of choices, including high-speed steel tools that work well. I would, however, use only ½″-shanked straight bits whose cutting diameters are under ⅞″.

Figure 4-13A

An ordinary router without an offset or oversized subbase is apt to tilt since only about 35 to 40 percent of the base plate is ever on the template while using a template collar.

Figure 4-13B

Joinery with the portable router should be done with an offset subbase (see the List of Suppliers on page 139). A downward force on the offset knob puts the pressure right on the work or template so the router stays flat at all times.

CUTTING TWO-FACED TENONS WITH THE JIG FOR END CUTS

1. Use a 42030 Porter Cable template collar guide and fixed-base router such as a Porter 690. Collet up a Jesada 880-516 and set its depth of cut to equal the length of tenon. **Caution:** Tenon faces less than ¾″ long and with shoulders less than ³⁄₁₆″ can be safely cut with 1½ hp fixed-base routers in one pass. If the stock removal is greater than this, cut the tenon in stages. The risk is not that the cutter may break or a motor overload—this cut is relatively safe in these regards. Rather, the problem is with the cutter-work engagement. If a cutter engages a lot of work in one pass, there is risk of kickback or loss of router control. So use common sense here and don't take big bites—even if you have the power and cutter strength to do so.

Figure 4-14
Rout both faces of the tenon. This collar system translates the cut line ⅛″ away from the template. Although this is a relatively long tenon, the shoulder is shallow enough, ⅛″, that it can be routed in one easy pass. Practice cutting tenons ½″ to ¾″ long by ⅛″ to ³⁄₁₆″ deep to get the feel of the process.

2. Index the work and position the template to equal the depth of shoulder plus ¼″. The ¼″ is to compensate for the differences in diameters of the cutter and collar. Rout the first cheek.

3. Reposition the work and rout the opposite face (Figure 4-14). Keep the router flat and the template guide collar against the template. A Porter Cable Offset Subbase 42193 will improve handling a lot here.

FOUR-FACED CENTERED TENONS

Woodworking jig-making is a very interesting science. In fact, I'm at the point now where jig-making and furniture-making have about the same appeal to me. I've designed and made a lot of jigs, and I've discovered that as a jig becomes more sophisticated, so do its capabilities. Fortunately, however, the task it's designed to do gets easier. For example, if you want to do a sweet but rather difficult job like making perfect four-faced centered 90° tenons, you'll find (at least in this chapter) the cutting of the tenon is very easy and requires little skill—but making the jig (a tenon maker) is a task requiring many skills.

There are a lot of ways to cut tenons with ordinary woodworking tools, but I have yet to see a nonproduction process produce tenons as pretty, as exact and as easy as the ones you'll be making with my tenoner/jig (Figures 4-15A and B). The jig is, of course, the heart of the process, but a plunge router, a few rabbet bits and a couple of bearings are also needed. The jig is an MDF platform/holder. The platform supports the router, which has a ski subbase on it to keep it from tipping into the window where the workpiece is accessed. The work-holding and indexing functions of the jig are met with an MDF panel and fence perpendicular to this platform

(Figures 4-16A and B). The tenon is formed by one or several trips around the work with a bearing-piloted rabbet bit. The lateral (east-west) depth of cut is determined by the cutter diameter and bearing, and the vertical (north-south) depth of cut is determined by your plunging depth. The whole affair is held fast either by the work or by clamping the fence in a vise.

Figures 4-15A and B

(Above; left) These tenons are really easy to make and take less than a minute to index, position and rout.

Figure 4-16A

The vertical panel and the fence provide the nest for the workpiece. I use a toggle clamp with a C-clamp to secure the work in the jig.

Figure 4-16B

The work is clamped on a penny. The window in the vertical panel is for more clamping access if needed.

The jig is small and portable. It can be made as sophisticated as you like or it can function quite well even if you cobble it together with a jigsaw, drywall screws and glue. My jig has been carefully template routed, joined and machine-screwed together. Jigs are evolutionary: The first one is usually an approximation—as your skills improve, so do your jigs. Let this first one be a learning experience and make the next one sweeter. Plan on cutting the windows out with a jigsaw or hand saw and do, by all means, use no. 8 or no. 10 drywall screws to hold it together.

As of this writing (June 1996), this jig is my invention and I'm the only one making them. If you're unwilling, unable or just too impatient to make one of my tenoners, you can order one from me (see the List of Suppliers on page 139).

Before starting out, read this entire section so you thoroughly understand the construction and just where you should make changes if you'd like to tenon larger stock. The nominal holding capacity of my jig is for stock to 2¼" thick, 6" wide and any length. There are off-the-shelf cutters and arbors to produce four-faced centered tenons with shoulders up to ⁹⁄₁₆" and lengths to 2½". (See Using the Tenoner, Step 4, on page 77.)

MAKING THE JIG FOR 90° USE

1. Cut two pieces of 3/4 MDF to 11" × 16⅝".
2. Cut windows in the panels as shown (Figure 4-17). They needn't be precise, because they are merely access windows. If the stock you plan to tenon is larger than 2¼" × 6", add the equivalent amount (in inches) over 2¼" × 6" to the window and panel dimensions, respectively (i.e., for stock over the 6" dimension, add to the

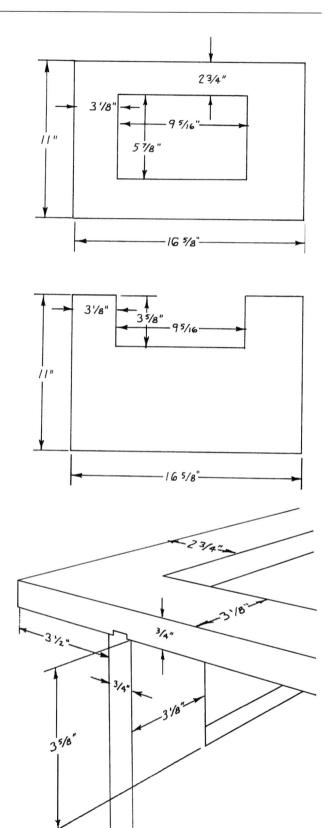

Figure 4-17
Drawings of panels and end view.

Figure 4-18
These panels must be at 90°. You may have to shim the corner braces to achieve a right angle. Do whatever it takes, as this is the only criticality in the jig.

long dimension of the window and panel).

3. Screw and/or T&G the panels together so the center line of the vertical panel is 3⅞″ from the edge of the horizontal panel, thus lining up the windows.

4. Reinforce as necessary with shopmade corner braces or machined right-angle aluminum or steel brackets. These panels must be at right angles (Figure 4-18).

5. Now make the fence from a piece of hardwood 1¼″ × 3½″ × 14″. Notch it as shown in the drawing (Figure 4-19) and fasten it to the panel with a ¼″-20 × 2½″ machine screw and nut. Put a second screw 7″ away from this one.

6. Before drilling the hole in the panel for the second screw, square the fence to the top (Figure 4-20). This hole is sloppy so you can adjust the fence to exactly 90° before tightening the nut. **Caution:** The fence always has to be well secured. Use three screws if necessary. If the fence should ever rotate while tenoning, you will spoil the work and perhaps have an accident. Check the security of the fence before each use.

7. Install a De-Sta-Co U-225 toggle clamp, centered, approximately 3½″ from the top of the fence (1½″ down from the notch). Use four no. 12 × 1¼″ pan-head sheet metal screws to fasten the fence.

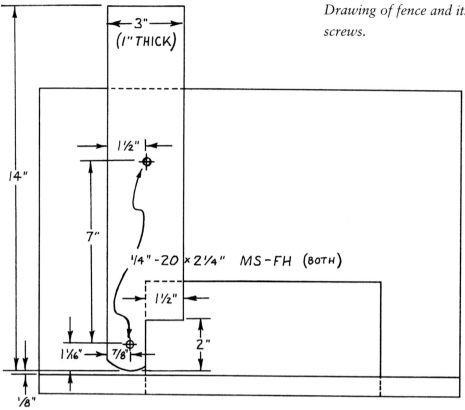

Figure 4-19

Drawing of fence and its location on panel with screws.

3"
(1" THICK)

14"

1½"

7"

¼"-20 × 2¼" MS-FH (BOTH)

1½"

2"

1 1/16"   7/8"

1/8"

Figure 4-20

Square the fence to the top panel as shown and clamp it in place. Use the hole in the fence as a guide to locate the hole to be drilled in the panel. Drill a 5/16" hole in the panel. I have a third screw in mine for more security. (I have a transfer punch in the hole.)

USING THE TENONER

1. Upend the jig on your workbench.

2. Place a penny on the bench, position the work on the penny against the fence and set the toggle clamp. Always use an additional C-clamp to clamp the work in the jig (see Figures 4-16A and B, page 73).

3. Invert the jig and secure in a vise (Figure 4-21). **Caution:** Make sure your work is held securely in the vise. Test your setup by pulling the jig back and forth before routing. When you're routing you will add 15 to 20 lbs. of weight and force to the system. If anything should slip, you could spoil the work or perhaps lose your balance and slip. The jig is very safe: I've made hundreds of perfect tenons in mine without any accidents. Knowing these few things beforehand should prepare you for any mishaps.

4. Collet up the rabbet bit and bearing that match your shoulder requirements. Use PRC

arbor TA-160-8XL and TA-222 (⅛″), TA-224 (¼″) TA-222 (⅜″) or TA-228 rabbet bits for the appropriate shoulder. Contact PRC (800-237-8613) for cutter and bearing specifics and set the depth to one-half the cutter height. Use a plunge router with a wide platform subbase that always straddles the window (Figure 4-22).

Figure 4-22
The complete setup. The work is indexed, secured and one penny's thickness lower than the work surface. The whole affair is clamped in the vise or on your beam, and the plunge router has a ski on it big enough that it'll span the window under all conditions.

Figure 4-21
The fence, either panel, or the workpiece can be clamped in the vise or on your bench beam. Be sure it's well secured before routing.

5. Now rout around the end of the work counterclockwise, finishing with the bearing against each face of the board. If only one, two or three faces are required, keep the cutter off the appropriate face(s). Lower the cutter one-fourth to one-half flute length, rout, and repeat to maximum depth (Figures 4-23A and B). If there should be any tear-out, try and climb cut, but take shallow cuts (⅜″ or less deep).

Figure 4-23A

During your final pass (for each depth of cut) make sure the bearing rolls on the faces of the stock to be routed. The surface of the work is the reference surface for the bearing. If you skip a spot you can't go back and cut it (at a new depth) again because the bearing will be rolling on the cheek, a nonreference surface.

Figure 4-23B

Close-up of bearing rolling on face of stock.

CHAPTER FIVE
Mortising With the Router

MORTISE BASICS

Mortising is so different from tenoning I decided to put it in its own chapter. As you know, mortises are square, round or rectangular holes made to receive a correspondingly shaped tenon. Tenons are cut entirely from the outside. The work can be presented on end or on the flat such that either the bottom or the side of the cutter makes the cut. The shoulder cuts are always square: There are no rounded corners on outside router cuts. The cutter always escapes the work (except on template-assisted cuts) so its radius is never recorded anywhere. It's impossible to ascertain the radius of a tool used to cut an outside cut (not so with an inside cut).

Mortises are entirely inside cuts that can only be addressed from the mortise face of the stock. The side of the flute always cuts the wall of the mortise, and the end of the router bit always cuts the bottom. Moreover, the inside corners are always rounded to the radius of the cutter doing the mortising. You must live with these facts if you want to mortise with a router.

The two router methods of mortising in this book use either the router table (open-ended mortises) or my "block-mortiser" and a hand router. We will make the mortiser, study the mortising cutters and rout some mortises.

ABOUT THE MORTISE

The mortise and tenon are an inclusive and dependent pair of joint members. One is useless without the other. The strength of the connection is a joint responsibility (no pun intended). If either member is poorly cut, the service of the joint is compromised. You should keep this in mind as you work through this chapter. It makes no sense to cut perfect tenons as you did in chapter four and then make less-than-acceptable mortises in this chapter.

Mortise and Tenon Uses

The mortise-and-tenon joint is one of the most important in cabinet- and furniture-grade situations. The joint is more commonly found in stick furniture (tables and chairs), but it can just as easily show up in paneled woodwork such as bookcases, dressers and cabinets. The mortise can occur on the ends of a stick or anywhere in between, and on any face. In panels, the mortises are often found receiving tenons near the long-grain edges, but shelving can be tenoned anywhere, all the way across the grain from top to bottom.

Mortise Anatomy

There are three center lines to a mortise: One center line is midway in depth, and the other two are midway in length and width. A tenon also has three center lines, but the nature of its function and shape have little to do with its creation or location. The positioning and the cutting of the mortise, on the other hand, are directly related to these center lines—and you must account for each one of them! The z axis (vertical depth of cut) is relatively easy to accommodate by plunging the cutter to the proper depth; it's of secondary importance. The center of the mortise (the intersection of the length and width center lines) can be located nearly anywhere on a workpiece—and herein lies half the adversity of mortising (Figure 5-1). The stick being mortised has three center lines of its own, and you have to line up the "cursors" so the mortise centroid (the intersection of its three axes) lands on the spot you've selected. Now, don't let the geometry scare you off: It's relatively easy to mortise the right-size excavation in the right place. I merely point all this out so you have a good definition of the problem before you let your router loose. Needless to say, you'll need a jig to help you position the mortise correctly and hold your work. Later on in this chapter I'll show you how to make the first evolution of a jig, and one, I must point out, with enough flexibility built into it to take care of a lot of mortises in a lot of different places. But first let's examine the mortising bit.

BITS FOR MORTISING

Mortising is possible only with straight bits. They can be spiral-ground, on-shear, straight up and down and of nearly any flute length. High-

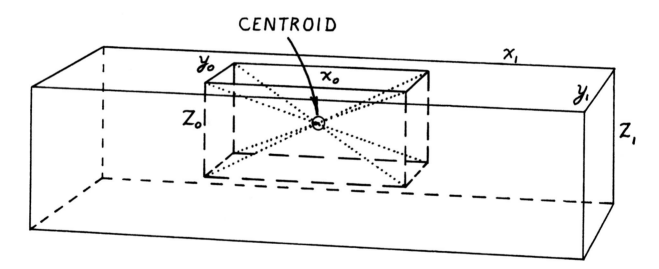

Figure 5-1

The centroid of the mortise is at the midlines of x, y and z. The centroid must lie on the center of the site you pick for it. It can occur most anywhere on the work. It's easy enough to say and lay out, but it's another matter to poke the hole in just the right place. The plunge router with its edge guides in tandem with the mortiser, when properly adjusted, can excavate the mortise right where you want it.

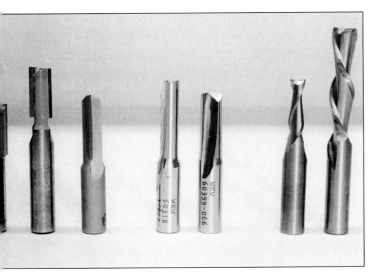

Figure 5-2

Any of these straight bits are capable of mortising. All solid carbide cutters (the two on the far right) are ground to plunge straight into the stock. Some cutters are more efficient than others but even high-speed steel does a great job.

speed steel, brazed-on carbide and solid-carbide bits can all mortise equally well (Figure 5-2). The sides of the flutes always cut, whether you hold the router still and push against the side of the mortise or sweep it down the length; it always cuts.

The end of the cutter doesn't always cut, and this can be hazardous. Some cutters are designed to plunge like a drill and cut during the plunge and during the sweep. These are true plunge cutters, and you should use only plunge-cutting bits for mortising. Some of these cutters are pointed, for boring right through the work; others are designed to cut a flat-bottom mortise (Figure 5-3). Ordinary straight bits cut on the bottom, but only if they're swept during and after the plunge. This will present a risk, because if you plunge without sweeping the router (a not-so-easy maneuver), the cutter will either burn up or find a spot (out of your control) where it can cut. This is especially challenging if you're cut-

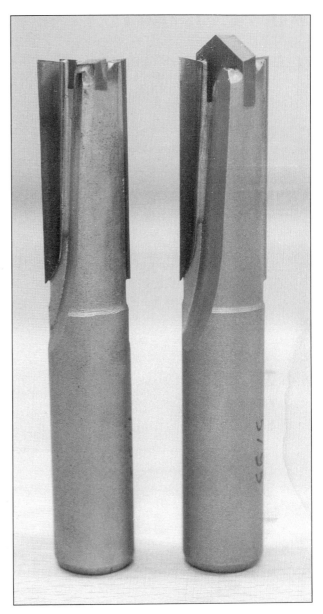

Figure 5-3

These two Wisconsin Knife Works cutters plunge straight through wood. The pointed boring end cutter is for through stock plunging and the other cutter is for blind flat-bottom work.

ting only one-cutter-diameter mortises. Router woodworkers worldwide cut mortises with nonplunging cutters—and you can learn to, too. However, there are, in my view, too many acceptable but practicable hazardous woodworking operations, and this is one I don't want my name associated with.

THE MORTISING FIXTURE

My mortiser (hereafter called a *block-mortiser* because of its blocky/chunky appearance) has seen five or six evolutions and could still stand a few changes—but it's pretty good. The tool consolidates many of the important demands of the process. A plunge router and two edge guides are required to use the jig. One or both of the edge guides can be shop-made. The capacity in section (of a workpiece) is from zero × zero to 1¾″ × 2¹⁵⁄₁₆″ × any length. You can mortise on any of the four faces of your work from end to end. If the capacity is under your requirements, I will point out the part and its dimension that needs changing to accommodate larger stock.

The block-mortiser consists of an *L-section* block (1), which the work is clamped to and the router slides on top of, a clamp block (2) screwed to the body of (1) with three toggle clamps and tapped holes for three jack screws, an auxiliary hold-down block—either screwed or glued to (1)—and two sliding stops. The toggle clamps secure the work to the fixture. The jack screws raise the work level with the top of the block and prevent the work from being dislodged during the downward force of the plunge. And the hold-down block allows you an

---

MORTISE CUTTER CHOICES

Nearly any straight bit can be used as a mortising tool, but you should consider the following when making the selection.

1. If you're cutting only one diameter, solid carbide should be a first choice. Almost all solid-carbide bits are plunging bits. The diameter selection is poor, but the length selection is good. They are very stiff, no matter what the diameter, and less likely to break in severe service.

2. Use a shank length commensurate with your depth requirements. Don't try to reach greater depths by inserting only the minimum length of shank into the collet. Buy longer-shanked tools for deeper cuts.

3. Mortising is demanding work. Most of the work is being done on the bottom ⅜″ of the tool. Short flutes with long shanks are better mortising tools than long flutes on short shanks because they cut better and they're less likely to break.

4. When cutting mortises greater than one cutter diameter, try to keep the cutter diameter to ½ or less of the mortise width. The more chopping room you give the cutter, the better.

5. Don't get overly concerned with flute design in your pursuit of selecting a cutter. Up-spiral cutters, for instance, aid in exhausting the chip from the mortise, all right, but most of the time the clutter of the baseplate, casting or other contrivance will impede the escape of the chip anyway. Better that you stop cutting periodically and vacuum out the chip.

6. Don't shy away from high-speed steel. If you match the cut rate with the feed rate, you can cut a lot of mortises before resharpening. Consider Wisconsin Knife Works' HSS steel bits, as they have plunge ability. Production mortising, however, will require carbide.

7. Consider single-flute bits. Most are stiffer than two-flute bits, they plunge better, and you can line them up to the scribe lines easier.

easy way to secure the jig (see Figures 5-4, 5-5 and 5-6). As the router travels left and right, the long dimension of the mortise is defined. The sliding stops accommodate mortises to about 5½″ long. The width of the mortise is controlled by the two edge guides.

Assembling the Mortising Fixture

The description that follows is for a screw-together assembly. Don't spend a lot of time on this first model: You will no doubt want to improve it as you gain experience. Make the second or third one sweeter; use this one as an experiment.

1. Cut and square up a 4½″ × 1¼″ × 24″-long piece of clear, straight-grained hardwood (oak, ash, walnut or beech, for instance). Add to the 4½″ dimension as needed for a workpiece mortised (on the edge) over 3″ (e.g., for work 3½″

wide add at least ⁹⁄₁₆″ to this dimension). This is the *router support block* (RSB).

2. Cut two pieces 1½″ square × 24″ and install ⁵⁄₁₆-18 T-nuts in each piece, centered and 3½″ from each end.

3. Screw each piece flush top and bottom and on the same side of the RSB. The flanges of all the T-nuts must be facing each other. The piece on the top is for added router support and to accept the bolts that lock the travel of the stops. The top piece we'll call the ARS, for *added router support*. The bottom piece we'll call the HDB, for *hold down block*. Use flathead no. 12 screws and penetrate the RSB to about 1″.

4. Cut a 1¼″ × 1⅝″ × 24″ *clamp block* (CB). Add, inch for inch, to the 1¼″ dimension for work over 1¾″ (e.g., if you are mortising the thin side—the edge—of a 2½″-thick stick, increase this dimension to 2″). Use three 225-U De-Sta-Co clamps on this piece to hold the

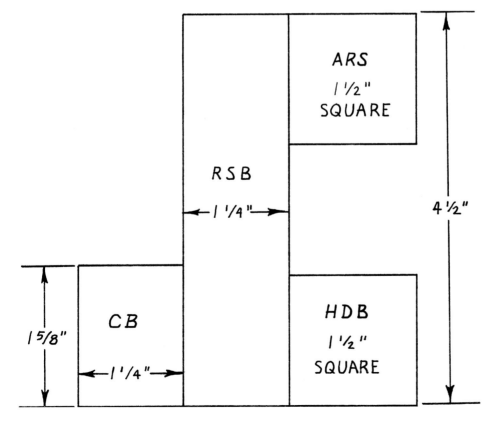

Figure 5-4
Drawing of the end view of the mortiser.

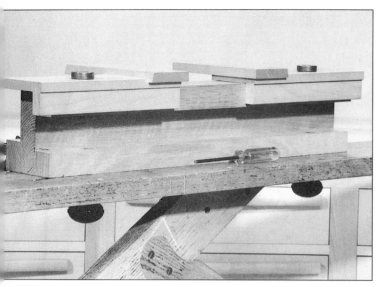

Figure 5-5

This is the back side of my mortiser. I've clamped it in place with two clamp knobs right through the bench.

work. Locate them on the 1⅝" face at 3½", 12" and 18½" from the left end. You may want to drill for a fourth clamp 1¾" from the right end. Sometimes I use this clamp for added support on a workpiece that is to be end mortised; at other times I clamp a stick under it for an index for the next workpiece (Figures 5-5 and 5-6).

5. Tap this piece or install ⁵⁄₁₆-18 T-nuts (flange up) 2" centered from each end and one in the center. Tap or drill through the 1¼" dimension. The ⁵⁄₁₆-18 thread is for the jack screws. These four pieces—the RSB, ARS, HDB and CB—could be T&Ged for added squareness and registration, but the whole unit will be just as strong and work just as well with a bunch of no. 12 screws holding it together. Keep in mind that a 225-U toggle clamp can press to 500 lbs., so three of them exert a lot of tear-apart force on the jig. Use at least six screws to hold the clamp block in place.

6. Now make the stops. These too can be screwed together. Although mine look nice, they're not that great. Make yours out of two pieces, as shown in the drawing. Just screw the pieces into an *L*-section. Cut an end-blinded 4"-long × ⁵⁄₁₆"-wide slot in each so the center of the slot lines up with the center of the T-nut in the ARS stick. Once you have them sliding nicely against the ARS, make sure the ends are 90° to the RSB long edge (Figure 5-7). Use

Figure 5-6

This is the front side of the tool. The three jack screws penetrate the bench, then pass through threaded holes in the clamp block and support the work. The two steel bars that hold the plunger on the center clamp have been shortened for edge guide clearance.

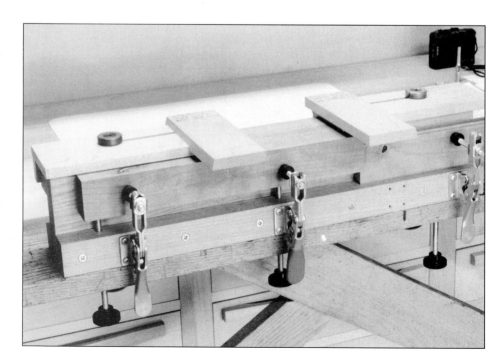

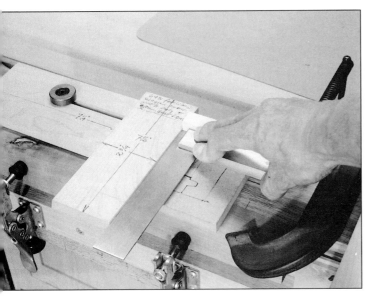

Figure 5-7
The work edge of the stop must be 90° to the work. Check them with a machinist's square. The dimensions are scribed on the stop.

$5/16$-18 × 2½" flathead machine screws and JFF-19305 flat-feet washers to secure the stops (Reid Tool).

7. Jack screws and clamp knobs: Make the jack screws and clamp knobs from $5/16$-18 all thread. Cut the clamp-knob rods to a length such that they go through your bench and all the way through the HDB T-nuts. Leave enough thread for a MPB-7 plastic clamp knob (Reid Tool). Drill access holes in your bench for these clamp knobs.

The jack screws should be 3" or 4" long. Their length is not critical. Use DK-131 knobs (Reid Tool).

8. Toggle clamps: Use three or four 225-Us (De-Sta-Co) as suggested. The middle clamp will interfere with most edge guides, so you will have to hacksaw some of the spindle holder off to allow clearance (see Figure 5-6). Use roundhead no. 10 or no. 12 sheet metal screws to fasten the clamps to the CB.

9. Edge guides: The nicest way to mortise is with an edge guide up against the work and another one to slide against the edge of the ARS. Edge guides define the width of the mortise and aid in keeping the router flat on such a relatively small surface. You'll need some long guide rods to be able to attach a second edge guide to the opposite side of the casting. I made a pair of fancy guides, but you needn't go to such extremes. Most edge guides can be used on both sides of the router: Just get longer rods and buy a second guide or make an *L*-section guide as shown (Figure 5-8). Drill the appropriate holes on the appropriate centers for your edge-guide rods. Secure the edge guide with two collars. (W.L. Fuller sells collars with hundreds of hole sizes.)

You now have the "makin's" for mortising, so square up some stock and lay out practice mortises. Try and scribe them close to the size of the tenons you made in chapter four.

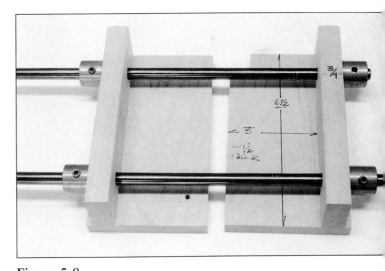

Figure 5-8
Handmade edge guides for the DeWalt 625 (also known as Elu 3338), shown here without a router for clarity. The dimensions scribed on the guide may or may not apply to your router, but at least you can use them for starters. The collars limit their position on the guide rods.

USING THE BLOCK-MORTISER

There are two fundamental ways of using the mortiser: One way assumes that you made your tenons to fit a mortise that is one cutter diameter in width; the other approach assumes that the mortises will be greater than a cutter diameter. As a rule, a one-cutter-diameter mortise is much easier to set up for and cut, but it's very hard on the cutter and often not as cosmetically presentable as mortises greater than a cutter diameter. The corners of a single-diameter-cut mortise are more difficult to chisel square, since the corner radii are usually harder to access and are larger. That aside, let's "cut to the chase."

Single-Cutter-Width Mortises

1. Scribe the north and south boundaries and one edge of the mortise on the work.

2. Set the toggle clamp spindles to the proper length and clamp the work in the jig so the long center line of the mortise is centered between the extremes of the sliding stops (Figure 5-9).

Figure 5-9
A scribe line on the center line of the maximum distance between the two slides (on the RSB) is a good starting point to line up with the center of the mortise on the work. A skinny workpiece was chosen here so you can see the jack screws in play.

3. Load up the router with the correct cutter and edge guides, and position the bit so it is tangential with the long scribe line (Figure 5-10).

4. Position the cutter tangent to the inside of both north and south cut lines and adjust the end stops (butt against router base and lock).

5. Set the plunge-router stops to cut as deep as your tenon is long. Start the motor, plunge, sweep and repeat to depth. Vacuum out the excavation from time to time, as there is really no easy way to get the chip out (Figure 5-11).

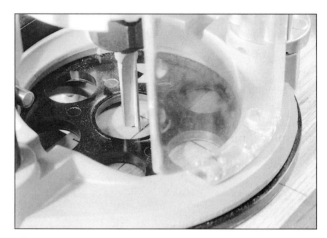

Figure 5-10
Single flute bits, like this WKW 68422, plunge satisfactorily, and one flute is easier to line up with a scribe line than a two-fluted design.

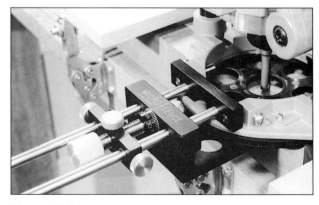

Figure 5-11
For one-cutter-diameter mortises like this one, only one edge-guide setting is necessary. The Wedler Microfence simplifies this adjustment enormously.

Mortising More Than One Cutter Diameter

You must lay out the entire perimeter for this mortise because the edge guides must be set for a slop. The slop is equal to the mortise width less one cutter diameter. Set the cutter tangent to all your scribe lines, and adjust the edge guides and stops so the cutter will stay within the confines of your lines (Figure 5-12).

Now plunge in the center of the mortise and waste away clockwise in the cavity. You will find that the cutter suffers most of its stress and strain in the center of the mortise where it is only cutting one diameter. As you approach the perimeter of the mortise, the cutter is taking less and less of a bite, and the walls of these mortises are therefore quite crisp (Figure 5-13).

To repeat the mortise on the next stick in the same place, merely index the work in the same place in the jig. You can position to a scribe line or butt the work against a stop. There is no need to lay out the mortises on subsequent pieces: The jig is already set up for all like mortises in equal-thickness material (Figure 5-14).

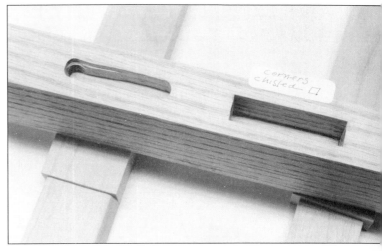

Figure 5-13

This mortise is much wider than the cutter so the router bit does some "swimming" before the guides come into play. The mortise on the left has not yet been resolved by the stops. The mortise on the right has been resolved. It always surprises me to see that the last 5 percent of the cut defines the outline of the whole thing. In single-diameter-cutter mortising there is no "freehanding" as the edge guide is always in play and the width of the mortise is evident from the first pass.

Figure 5-12

With this mortise (more than one cutter diameter in width) two edge guides are in play.

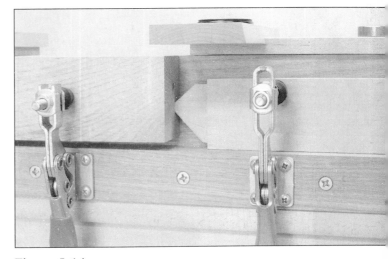

Figure 5-14

Once I've set up the coordinates for the mortise on my mortiser I use a stop to locate the workpiece. Each subsequent workpiece is butted against the stop and held with at least two toggle clamps.

DEEP THROUGH MORTISES

If you have a lot of mortises to do, waste away most of the mortise by drilling it out on the drill press before routing. If your mortises are right through the stock, you can rout only half the way through, or as deep as practical, and then drill out the remainder of the waste, staying inside the mortise confines. Working from the waste side of the mortise, rout the area clean with a flush-trimmer bit whose bearing is on the end of the cutter (Figure 5-15). Mortises through 3″ or 4″ stock are routable with this tactic.

SQUARING THE CORNERS OR ROUNDING THE TENON

As you no doubt have discovered, the insertion of the tenon in the mortise is confounded by the round corners of the mortise. You can either round over the corners of your tenons or chisel out the corners of the mortise. Corner chisels are available for this, as are rasps and files to round over the tenons (Figure 5-16).

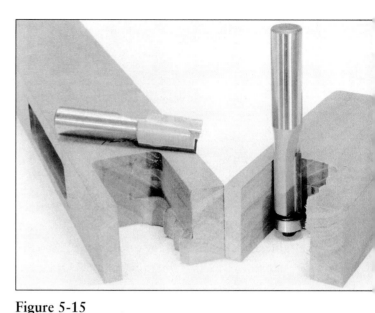

Figure 5-15
I have band-sawn into the interior of this mortise. The top half of the mortise was machined in the mortiser. Then I drilled the rest of the way through roughly on the drill press. I used the trimmer cutter on half the mortise from the opposite side and I left some of it rough. The laparotomy (a cutaway view) is shown with the appropriate cutters.

Figure 5-16
The corners of these mortises were squared up with the corner chisels shown. You can round the corners of the tenon if you'd rather. It is impossible to rout the corners of a tenon round, all the way to the shoulder, without a template.

OPEN-ENDED MORTISES ON THE ROUTER TABLE

Open mortises on the end of a stick are quite manageable on the router table. I would never blind-mortise on the table, as that would require me to lower the work onto a live cutter. I strongly advise that you follow my example.

Open-ended mortises are quite safe, and I do them all the time—especially when preparing for sliding dovetail mortises. The mortises I cut on the table are always one cutter diameter. Widening slots (mortises) on the table can lead to accidental and dangerous climb cuts that will snatch the work right from your hands. Single-diameter cuts are immune to such calamities.

The safest way to cut open-ended mortises is to extend the cutter to the final depth and place a pile of ³⁄₁₆"-thick spacers on the table, removing one for each depth of cut. The sequence is as follows.

STEP 1   Position end stop B, and center the cutter left and right with the fence (Figure 5-17).

STEP 2   Hold the work down and against the fence. Feed at a uniform rate consistent with the cutting rate of the tool (Figure 5-18).

STEP 3   You should stop the motor after each pass unless you have a safe and practical way to remove each layer of plastic without touching the cutter (Figure 5-19).

Figure 5-18
This is my second pass. As I remove each layer of plastic the cutter takes another modest ¼" cut.

Figure 5-17
The end stop is clamped to the fence to limit the work's travel. With this much cutter extension it should be clear that the cut must be taken in steps. Five pieces of ¼" plastic will take care of that.

Figure 5-19
The final pass defines the length, depth and width of the mortise. There is a lot of cutter engaged in the work here. If the work is not square or if your router table and fence are not flat you are at risk of a kickback. Get your feet wet with shallow mortises on scrap first.

MORTISING FOR LOOSE TENONS

The loose-tenon mortise-and-tenon is a rough abbreviation of the classical mortise-and-tenon. Both halves of the joint are mortised and then joined with a loose and separate tenon, like a spline (Figure 5-20). There are many possible configurations for this, including blind-mortising both pieces so the tenon is completely hidden. The chief advantages of the system are the elimination of the tenon-making step and its jigs and the simplification of the mortising setups. The disadvantages are the added hassle of making tenon stock and a sacrifice of strength. (An integral tenon, being part of the stock itself, is nearly impossible to extract from the end of a stick in tension. A loose tenon, albeit perfectly seated and glued in the long grain of a rail, has nowhere near the same pull strength. Nevertheless the joint is serviceable and practical.)

In my approach here, both pieces of the joint are open-mortised (on the table), so its application is restricted to end-of-stick-tenoning connections such as doors and Parson's table legs and rails. In spite of its simplicity and relative lack of strength, the joint is by no means trivial. I've seen, for example, 100 lb. entry doors joined in this way, although I think it would be prudent to use two tenons (equally spaced) for each joint and perhaps a little hardware.

CUTTING THE JOINT AND UNDERSTANDING THE PROCEDURE

Both joint members are cut in the safest way— on the router table. Each piece is cut with the work flat or on edge; no cuts are made with the stock held on end (vertical). The cuts should be made as deep as is practical, as penetration is vital for glue surface and strength. The mortise width should be about one-third the thickness of

Figure 5-20
Two examples of loose tenons in their mortises. I wonder about the origin of the term "loose," as these splines are well fixed after gluing.

the rail stock and only one cutter width. The tenon stock (spline) should be produced from the planer and then routed as necessary to nest in the radius produced from the mortise cutter.

Cutting the Mortises

1. Select the cutter and position the table fence for a centered cut on the rail. Achieving exact centering is unnecessary because both pieces will be referenced from common edges and will line up no matter what (Figure 5-21).

Figure 5-21

If you don't want to get mixed up with a lot of fancy measuring, this is the joint for you. I ground this ¼" rod to a point. A scribe line marks the center of the cut. Line up the point with the scribe line, then lock the fence, change cutters and rout to depth.

Figure 5-22

The final pass. The workpiece on the right has had its surgery. The other workpiece is on the operating table stuck on the cutter against the plastic stop. The cuttings in rails are round-ended but flat-bottomed.

2. Extend the cutter to final depth and stack up ³⁄₁₆"- or ¼"-thick pieces of Masonite or plastic to raise the work so that only a cut of ¼" (or less) is possible.

3. Set a stop to limit the workpiece travel, and rout all the rail stock to full cutter depth × 1½"- to 2½" long (Figure 5-22).

4. Now rout the leg (or stile) material. Keep the cutter at the same depth of cut and adjust the fence if necessary. (If the leg and rail stock are the same thickness, no adjustment is necessary.) The length of workpiece travel should be equal to the cutter depth (e.g., if the cutter extension is 1¼", the work travel should be 1¼"). Rout all the leg stock (Figure 5-23).

Figure 5-23

Due to its position on the table during the cut, the leg (or stile) stock mortise is square-ended, but the bottom is round. The joint is misaligned (but assembled) for clarity.

MAKING THE TENON STOCK

The tenon (spline) stock has to be sawn, planed and routed twice to fit the mortises. The end should be routed before chopping to length. You can take spare material and cut it to length as necessary. The spline stock needn't be the same species as the project stock, but it's not a bad idea to use scrap and odd cutoffs from your job, as this material will have the same equilibrium moisture content (EMC).

1. Joint and plane some material to a thickness consistent with a slip fit in the mortise. (**Note:** You may wish to experiment here since these joints seem to swell more than an ordinary mortise and tenon.

2. Rip to a width equal to the cutter extension used to cut the mortises plus about 1/64".

3. Now, before cutting to length, round the end of stock to the same radius as the cutter used to make the mortises. A bullnose bit is the best choice of cutter. Using the router table and

miter gauge is one way to make the cross-grain cut. If the stock is too long to handle safely on the table, it can be routed with the hand router, template and template collar (Figure 5-24).

4. With the same cutter in the router table, rout just less than a full radius (so some uncut section of the stock is always against the fence) on one edge (Figure 5-25).

5. Chop to length less about 1/64" for glue space (Figure 5-26).

Figure 5-25
Rout the edge round on the router table. A bullnose bit makes the cut in one pass, or the equivalent round-over bit does it in two. Leave about 1/16" or more of uncut material to ensure that the cut is uninterrupted.

Figure 5-24
Round the end grain of the tenon stock before chopping to length with a 1/4" round-over (PRC TA-204, for example). I've trapped the miter gauge blade between two 3/8"-thick pieces of MDF to assure parallel travel past the cutter.

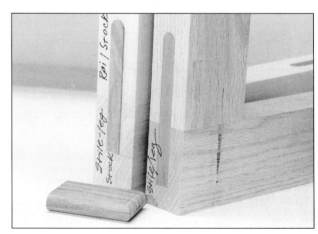

Figure 5-26
The spline is about 1/64" proud in height; sand it flush after gluing. Leave one edge square and round the other. One end should also be rounded to nest with the end of the rail socket.

REINFORCING THE JOINT

Sometimes routed joints are such that they need reinforcement. Small-diameter bits can't cut very deep, and the largest slotters will never compete with even small-diameter saw blades. There will be occasions, whether due to tool bit design, power requirements or safety, that router-cut joints could use some help. Here are three techniques I use that can transform a borderline joint into an unbreakable one.

The Corner Brace

In a corner leg-and-rail configuration, the corner brace will compensate nicely for short or otherwise compromised tenons. The brace should be cut so its long grain travels from rail to rail. Rout a 90° notch out of the triangle so you can drill it for big screws (Figure 5-27).

The Mending Batten

This can be used in shallow mortise-and-tenon joints where the cutters can't penetrate deep enough for a strong joint (Figure 5-28).

The Steel Cross Dowel

If the head of a bolt can be tolerated or perhaps covered, it can be driven through a leg and into a threaded steel cross dowel. The tension in the bolt will hold two pieces of wood together nicely. Drill the hole for the bolt with the joint registered and clamped together. The bolt should penetrate the second piece by at least an inch. For heavy-duty work, the penetration should be 2″ or 3″. The hole for the cross dowel should be slightly oversize to allow for easy alignment (Figure 5-29).

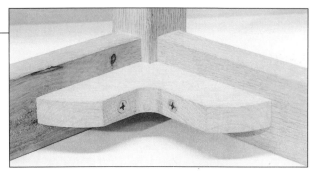

Figure 5-27
I routed a notch out of the hypotenuse of the triangle so I could drill it easier. I also cut a rabbet at the apex so the brace will cope around the leg.

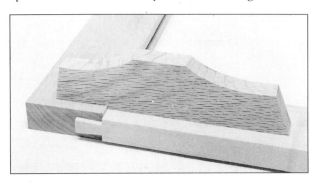

Figure 5-28
The rail is thinner than the stile so I wasted the end of the batten to match and fit the difference. You can glue and screw and even T&G the batten to the rail for an indestructible connection. Put the batten on the hidden side of the assembly or pretty it up and use it as a design feature on the front side.

Figure 5-29
This joint is only ⅛″ deep and would never hold together without some hardware. This cross dowel is located in the face of the stock; it can also be positioned through an access hole drilled on-edge.

CHAPTER SIX
Routing Sliding Dovetails

SLIDING-DOVETAIL BASICS

Sliding dovetails are very similar to tongues, grooves, mortises and tenons. The socket (also known as a *way*) has the same function as a groove or mortise, and the dovetail is equivalent to the tenon or tongue. The mortise and tenon and tongue and groove are always straight-sided cuttings, and each member of those joints can be accessed by and created with straight bits. Tongues and grooves can be stopped (not visible from the outside) or through. Mortises likewise can be blind or through, and they can also start

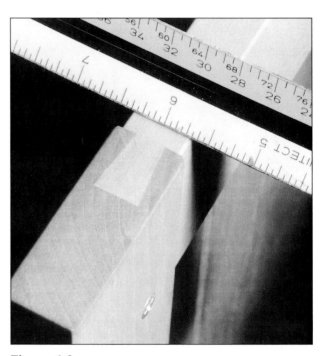

Figure 6-2
The dovetail in this door is acceptable, but a narrower, longer dovetail would be better.

Figure 6-1
In Figures 1, 2 and 3 the dovetail is accessible from only one end of the way. The so-called French dovetail in this drawer is also stopped.

Figure 6-3
The dovetails in this leg are quite satisfactory. A longer and skinnier cutter would be ideal, but such a cutter does not exist.

at the edge or end of a board. Sliding dovetails, as described in this chapter, will have access to and be open to at least one end of the way (Figures 6-1, 6-2 and 6-3). Members of either sex are also cut with the same tool.

DOVETAIL ANATOMY

The fit of a dovetail is critical because of its taper. While it is possible for different-length dovetails to fit in the same socket (Figure 6-4), the best fit is achieved when there is a 3- or 4-mil space (the thickness of a dollar bill) between the bottom of the way and the end of the tenon, and a 1- to 3-mil space between the walls of the socket and the tenon cheeks. In the tenon-making process, each vertical depth-of-cut change narrows the neck of the tenon (if the fence position remains the same)—and herein lies the difficulty in the cut and fit of the joint. There are strategies to overcome this, and I'll tell you about them in a minute, but first let's look at the application and advantages of this joint.

APPLICATIONS AND BENEFITS OF SLIDING DOVETAILS

Whenever a mortise and tenon is called for at the end of a stick, a sliding dovetail can apply: cabinet doors and legs and rails, for example. Dovetails can also work nicely as aprons for cabinets, and because of their excellent pull strength, they work well in drawers. There is no reason they can't be used in shelves, dividers and drawer blades. A dovetailed batten can flatten an unsupported panel, and for the same reason, dovetails can be used as bread-boarded ends on table or desk tops.

Dovetail tenons and sockets are great because the taper locks the work together and facilitates assembly. If a joint is well made, it will outlast the glue that sticks it together. Furthermore, it is possible and sometimes essential to assemble a dovetail without any glue at all! A batten, for instance, is in cross-grain—if it is glued, it will split the panel it resides in, due to seasonal dimensional changes.

DESIGNING THE JOINT

The routed dovetail joint is obviously limited to the availability and design of the dovetail bit. Fortunately, makers of commercial dovetail jigs have expanded their repertoire. There are now dozens of diameters, lengths and tapers to choose from. On the other hand, these cutters were all made for relatively shallow use in carcasses and boxes that are normally much thinner than legs and rails are wide. What this means is that you can't make a tenon longer than 1¼" (as of September 1996). For ordinary work this is usually acceptable, but for large-scale projects like timber-frame joinery or entryway doors, the routed dovetail is undersized.

The criteria for a good dovetail joint include angle, penetration and interference; they're all interrelated. The penetration of the tenon into its way should be as deep as practical, but will always be dictated by available cutter length. For tenons that enter the two adjacent faces of a leg,

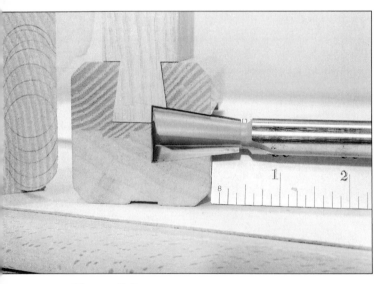

Figure 6-5
This leg-and-rail system represents a reasonable compromise between penetration and interference. The cutter is ⅜" longer than the tenon. So, at full depth, you can see there would just be too much interference.

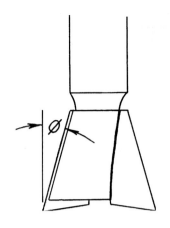

Figure 6-6
The angle of a dovetail bit is measured from the vertical axis (parallel to the shank). As the angle (theta) increases, so does the steepness. The steeper the angle the more the pull strength, provided you don't rout too close to the edge.

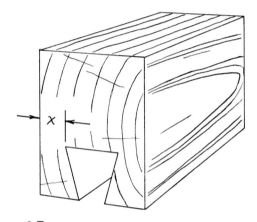

Figure 6-7
X *indicates the minimum material in a centered female member for a strong joint.*

you must also consider just how much the sockets may interfere with each other (Figure 6-5).

Lone tenons in the ends of rails, for example, have no interference problems and are easy to design for. Again, the length should be as long as possible and as narrow as practical. The steeper the angle (Figure 6-6) of a dovetail bit, the greater its pull strength. However, you should design this and other dovetail joints so you leave about 25 to 30 percent (or more) of the thickness of the way member at each side of the tenon at the base of the tenon (Figure 6-7).

Dovetails spread as they penetrate, cutters are short, and interference is common. However, dovetails are so important that we should learn to live with their liabilities; your woodwork will last longer with dovetails, and there are usually simple countermeasures, such as those for mortises and tenons, available to you to strengthen dovetail joints (see chapter five).

DOVETAIL CUTTERS

There are a lot of dovetail cutters in production today. They are made from either high-speed steel (HSS) or brazed-on carbide. There are no solid-carbide cutters because the cost of grinding them is prohibitive. As a rule, dovetail cuttings are of short duration and path length. Because of this, high-speed steel is acceptable. However, the cuttings are full-depth, one-pass cuts and can be abusive if some of the waste is not pre-plowed away. Consequently, the industry has chosen carbide over steel, and the overwhelming number of cutters available are carbide-faced steel (Figure 6-8).

The angles for dovetail bits run from about 2° to 3° for shallow, easy-lock stuff like stair treads, to 6° to 14° for ordinary work and dovetail jigs, and to steep angles of 17° to 20° for spe-cialized joinery or machine applications. For a given angle, there are often different flute lengths and diameters. Keep an eye out for very narrow-necked cutters; sometimes the manufacturer grinds so deeply into the shank that the cutter can't possibly cut without chattering. In my view, no less than .200″ of steel should remain in the shank (Figure 6-9).

Dovetail cutters can only be used at one depth (vertical) in the way. If you don't like the cut in the work you've just made, you obviously can't cut any shallower—but you can't cut any deeper either (the succeeding cut will be spoiled by the cut before it). Because of this phenomenon, there will be times when you will have to pre-waste a pathway with a straight bit so the dovetail bit won't be so stressed by taking the whole pathway in one pass. For me, most cuts over about ⅜″ deep require a pre-waste operation. Incidentally, tenon cuts can often tolerate a deeper second or third dovetail cut, but tenon cuts are so easy on the cutter that this option is only of concern during the calibration phase (setup cuts) of the cuttings.

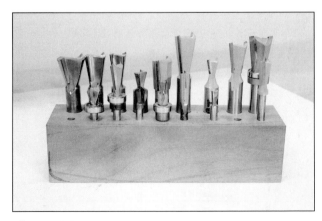

Figure 6-8
I have fifteen or twenty dovetail bits. When I design a dovetail joint I choose the cutter by eyeballing its profile on the stock. If I can't find the right tool, I'll probably mortise and tenon.

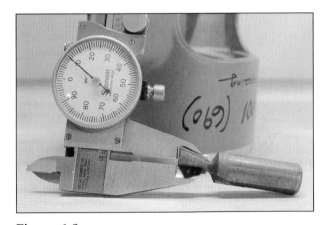

Figure 6-9
This quite ordinary 14° dovetail bit has just about ⅛″ of material left in its shank and web after the grinding process. It will bend, flex and chatter the walls of the dovetail sockets it cuts.

ROUTING THE WAYS

I will cover two methods of routing ways: One approach is on the router table and the other is with the hand router. In both cases the cutter selection is critical to the design of the joint (as previously mentioned) and the safety and the simplification of the cutting operations. If the socket (the way) is only one cutter width, there is no danger of an accidental climb cut, and the cut is achieved in *one pass with one setup*. This greatly simplifies the cut-and-fit process, and you now have a target for making the pin (the tenon); the pin will be the same size as the cutter.

CUTTING SOCKETS WITH THE HAND ROUTER

Sockets cut with the hand router are done only on wide stock (e.g., drawer fronts or cabinet sides) because cutting them on the router table is problematic. (Panels don't stay flat, the chip fouls the cutter pathway, you can't see the cutter and large panels can't be handled well on the

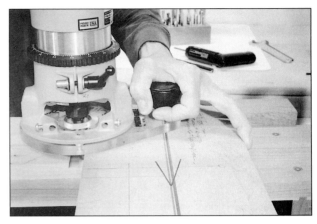

Figure 6-10
With my spidery fingers pulled over the left edge of the template I'm sure to keep the collar against the right side. This also helps keep the machine flat on the template. Let the knob track the black line parallel to the edge. This keeps the same section (radian) of the collar always against the template.

table.) For cuts deeper than about ⅜″ (or shallower if the cutter chatters and strains), a straight-cutter pre-plow should precede the dovetail bit cut. The smart way to make the cut is with a template and two routers, each with a collar with the same diameter on the subplate. This

---

DOVETAIL SAFETY CONSIDERATIONS

1. Be sure and prepare your material accurately before dovetailing. There will be occasions when squareness is acutely important, especially on the router table.

2. The dovetail bit is completely trapped in the work in way-making. If the work or the router should teeter, kickback may occur. Square material and a fence that is square to the tabletop will minimize this risk. An offset subbase will aid in keeping the router flat in portable applications.

3. A cutter jam may pull the cutter from the collet. If a jam should occur, check to ascertain if the cutter has changed its depth of cut before proceeding. Furthermore, find out *why* it occurred.

4. Widening dovetail ways can be hazardous. You may unwittingly climb cut and have the work pulled from your hands. In all my examples, I rout only one cutter diameter. I never widen a socket.

5. Always pre-rout as much waste as possible with a straight bit before cutting the ways with the dovetail bit.

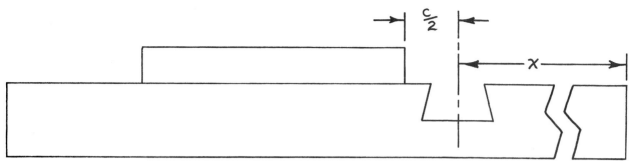

Figure 6-11

(Above) This drawing illustrates the relationships of the template, the center line of the cutter, and the end of the board. For example, for a cut to fall on the 10" centerline with a 1" collar in play, position the template 10" plus ½" from the end of the board.

Figure 6-12

This dovetail (stopped mortise) was preceded by a series of straight bit cuts. Even a big dovetail bit like this might break off if thrust into a workpiece without a pre-routed tunnel. If you wobble the work, you'll tear the walls of the pathway, burn the profile or kick back the work.

tactic facilitates the cutting since both routers will be cutting on the same center and only one setup is needed for both cuts.

You'll need a right-angle template for this procedure (see page 58). Use ⅜"- or ½"-thick MDF. The template should be an inch or more longer than your work is wide. The working edges of the template must be straight and free of any defects, as these will be copied onto your work. The angle of the cleat should be adjusted with a machinist's square to exactly 90°.

For best results, an offset subbase (e.g., a Porter Cable 42193) and a fixed-base router should be used. The subbase will keep the router flat on the template, and you can easily pull on the knob so the template collar is always against the template (Figure 6-10).

Hand Routing Sockets

1. Install a Porter Cable 42030 template collar (for cutters to ¾" in diameter) or a 42021 (for cutters to 1") on your subbase and collet up the appropriate cutter(s). Set the final depth of cut. (Final depth of cut equals desired cutting depth plus one template thickness.)

2. Position the template. Its edge should be at a distance equal to the distance from the center line of the cut plus ½ the collar diameter from the end of the stock (Figure 6-11).

3. Pre-plow, if necessary, with a straight bit,

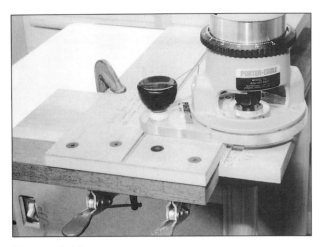

Figure 6-13

I put two toggle clamps on the template for easy clamping. A C-clamp at the corner is there for insurance against an accidental slip. Routing from this side of the cut helps keep the collar and cutter tracking against the fence.

smaller in diameter than the dovetail cutter's minimum diameter (Figure 6-12).

4. Now rout the way (Figure 6-13).

ROUTING SOCKETS FOR LEGS AND STILES

These cuttings are usually short, 2″ to 4″, and since the stock is much too narrow to hand-rout, the cuttings are done on the router table. The process is essentially the same as routing open-ended mortises with one exception: After the pre-plow routing, the straight bit is exchanged for a dovetail cutter, and that cut is done on the same center but in one pass.

Cutting Leg and Stile Sockets

1. Select a straight bit smaller in diameter than any diameter of the dovetail profile in the cut. (A dovetail cutter has a major diameter, the *cutting diameter*, at its end, and a minimum diameter where it meets the shank.)

2. Rout all of the stock with the straight bit to the depth you will cut the dovetail, less ¹⁄₁₆″.

3. Change cutters and rout the dovetail in one pass. Make no fence changes and feed the stock only from right to left (Figure 6-14).

ROUTING DOVETAIL TENONS

There are a lot of ways to cut dovetail tenons. In my view, the safest way is to cut them with the hand router and the jig for on-end cuts (described in chapter four). Dovetail tenons are anatomically the same whether they fit into a drawer face or a table leg. They can interfere with each other, however, in a leg-rail connection—we'll deal with that later on. For the most part, dovetail tenons are cut the same way as two-faced straight tenons, using a collar, a template and a fixed-base router.

By making the sockets (ways) first and making them only one cutter width, you have substantially simplified the process. The goal now is to make the tenon the same size as the cutter and as long as the socket is deep.

Figure 6-14

The dovetail cutter is set about ¹⁄₁₆″ deeper than the preplow. This maneuver will aid in its tracking as the end of the cutter is now trapped in its own new pathway.

Cutting the Tenons

Begin by gathering up everything you used in chapter four to make two-faced tenons on end, only this time collet up the same dovetail bit you used to cut the mating socket. (Since this is an outside cut, you can use an equal-angle cutter with a larger diameter if desired.) A Porter Cable 42021 collar will allow access to any production-made dovetail bit. The largest cutter today (as of July 1997) is $13/16''$ in diameter. As before, an acrylic offset subbase and collar guide system is the best to use because you can see what you're cutting, keep the tool flat on the template and pull the collar against the template without any loss of control (Figure 6-15). A 6″-round base with a 1″ template collar in play has no more than 42 percent of its area on the work, and before the collar comes in contact with the template edge, only 30 to 35 percent of a round base plate is on terra firma!

1. Index (position) the work against the fence and up against the template. Adjust the cutter extension to equal the depth of the socket and the thickness of the template minus the thickness of a dollar bill (Figure 6-16).

2. Position the template so the first cut produces some shoulder. (Remember: The dovetail you're trying to cut will be the same size as the dovetail cutter you're using.)

Figure 6-16
A good first approximation of the depth of cut can be made upside down, as shown. Use a scrap piece of the same thickness as the template stock to account for the template.

Figure 6-15
This arrangement is ideally suited to single-depth edge cuts like this one. A round base would be at risk on edge work: The tool teeters easily, since more than half the weight is supported by you, not the work. A collar guide shifts the router past the center even more.

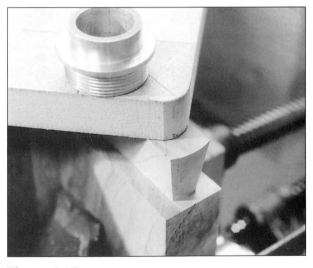

Figure 6-17
I've repositioned the work for the third shoulder. I rounded the corner of the template a little so the cut won't be so square.

Figure 6-18
The fit.

Figure 6-19A
Trace the cut (roughly) from the overlap of the two tenons in their mortises.

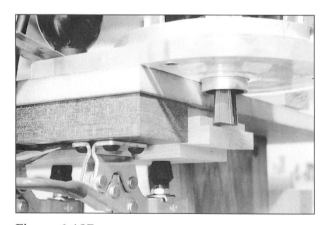

Figure 6-19B
Make a calibration cut and test the fit. Before undoing the setup scribe a line on the work against the template so you know the starting position of the template.

3. Flip the work over and repeat the cut. Try the fit. If incorrect, raise or lower the cutter or move the template as necessary. When the fit is correct, make at least two spare tenons.

4. To completely cover the dovetail socket, a third shoulder on the tenon is required. You may hand-saw it or you may reposition the work to rout it (Figures 6-17 and 6-18).

TENON INTERFERENCE

Due to the taper of a dovetail tenon, there is a likelihood that the tenons in a leg (especially a square leg) will interfere with each other (see Figure 6-3 on page 94). If they do, you'll need to cut a dovetail notch in one of the tenons. This could be done on the router table, but a more exact approach is to use the hand router and a template. Cutting the notch the right size on the first try is nearly impossible; don't even try it unless you've made plenty of spare test tenons. It's not very hard to get it right: just start by taking an undersize cut, and then test fit, adjust and cut again. Use the same cutter and collar that you used to make the tenons.

Cutting Dovetails to Accommodate Interference

1. Position the template with the stock flat, and set the cutter height to your best approximation (Figures 6-19A and B).

2. Reposition the template and/or change the depth of cut based on your considerations of the fit. A change in cutter height will automatically widen the cut without a change in template position. So if the first notch is close, a cutter-height change alone may do it.

3. On my third try, I got the right combination (Figures 6-20A and B).

Figure 6-20A
I got the fit correct.

Figure 6-20B
I made a little rabbeted cut-off to reference off the end of the work for the correct placement of the template on the next piece.

ASSEMBLY TIPS

Sliding-dovetail assembly can be difficult because dovetails have a tendency to jam and wedge, and there's a lot of glue mess.

1. Don't try to put the whole assembly together in one shot.

2. Do pretest the fit of every joint.

3. Assemble, glue and clamp one corner at a time. If your cuts and fittings are good, they'll stick together nicely (in warm weather, 70+ °F) in a half an hour or so. Then do the opposite corner.

4. A right-angle corner brace will keep the corner square during the glue-up (Figure 6-21).

5. For less of a mess, apply glue only to the bottom half of the socket and the top half of the tenon.

Figure 6-21
Use a corner brace (cut from 6"-wide material) to square up the work before clamping. To minimize assembly problems you can glue up a corner at a time.

CHAPTER SEVEN

Commercial Dovetail and Finger-Joint Jigs

Dovetail jigs and fixtures are indeed important accessories in the router-joinery arena. I like them, but I don't use them. I like a challenge, and my challenge has always been to develop new ways of joining rather than to surrender to the template-jig fixtures. I think this approach has paid off for me, because I've learned a lot more about assembly and joinery. For me, choosing the "jig" closes the gate on alternative joint and assembly design. This, of course, may not apply to you, especially since the art of routing is really one of expedition.

Dovetail- and box-joint jig hardware comes in two designs: One arrangement has the work fixtured while the cuttings are portably routed; the other design fixtures the router while the work is driven over the cutter. Six major systems are battling it out today. Two of them use the router table and the other four use templates and hand routers. Each system has its advantages. For me, the hand-routed approach has the most appeal because it's easier to zing in and out of a template comb with a router in hand than to slide the work a pin at a time over a cutter on the router table. Furthermore, a table system means you have to have a nice router table, whereas the template systems are essentially ready for work right out of the box.

THE OMNIJIG

The Omnijig (Figure 7-1) is a template system in which the work is clamped to the same heavy hardware that the template is fixtured to. The hand router is used for all the cuts. The unit is capable of half-blind or through dovetails (see Figures 7-9A–D). It also can be used for sliding tapered dovetails as well as box joints. All the

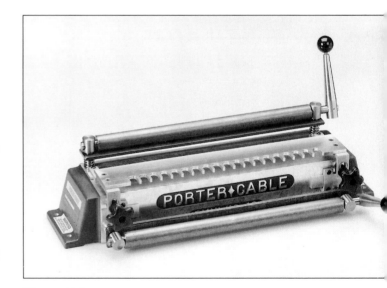

Figure 7-1

The 16" Porter Cable Omnijig was derived from the fixed centered dovetail jigs. It is a heavy-duty tool with robust clamps and sturdy aluminum templates. It does through and sliding tapered dovetails and many other joints (photo supplied by Porter Cable).

joints are used with collar guides; there are instances, though, where bearing-guided cutters can be used.

The clamping system is the heaviest-duty of all the systems, easily flattening wayward sticks. The widest jig can handle material to 24″ wide and 1″ thick. Once the unit is set up for a specific joint, succeeding projects using the same joinery require few changes. This is also true of the other systems. Through dovetail spacing can be arranged to suit your needs, but the half-blind dovetails and finger joints are on fixed centers. The sockets made with the adjustable template are restricted to one cutter width.

THE LEIGH JIG

The Leigh Jig is also a template system, but the spacing and width of dovetail pins and sockets produced from it can be more than one cutter width (never less).

The Leigh Jig (Figure 7-2) is regarded as the most versatile. It is capable of through, half-blind and sliding dovetails on stock up to 1½″, depending on the template system used. Box joints and multiple-carcass mortises and tenons are also possible. The system uses a portable router and a new, patented, tapered template collar guide system for all its joints (Figure 7-3). A twist of the guide positions the collar lower or higher in the template, increasing or decreasing the cutter travel slightly. This in turn affects the fit of the joint.

The Canadian manufacturers have gone to great lengths to ensure their tooling is compatible with most routers, template guide systems and off-the-shelf cutters. This much versatility does come with some degree of setup challenge, however. Although the owner's manuals are long and comprehensive, the manufacturers are constantly working on ways to simplify.

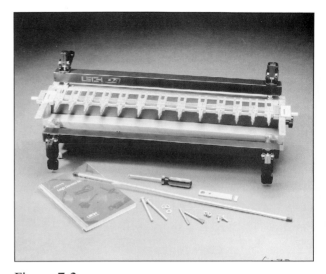

Figure 7-2
The Leigh jig is the most comprehensive of all the dovetail systems. It is fully adjustable and includes its own cam-lock work clamps (photo supplied by Leigh).

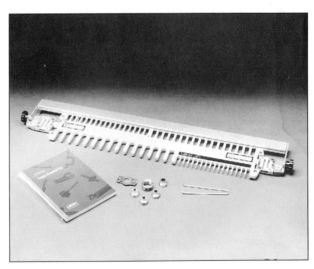

Figure 7-3
The Leigh finger joint template is used with the collar guide system in the foreground. The collar guide is tapered 5° so as you rotate it in its threaded holder its effective diameter (in contact with the template) changes. This in turn changes the cutter travel between the tines of the template (photo supplied by Leigh).

THE KELLER JIG

The Keller Jig is yet another template system and is often cited as being the simplest to use (Figures 7-4 and 7-5). The heavy, indestructible CNC-produced aluminum plate templates are designed for fixed-centered use, although they can be repositioned for variable spacing, if desired. The templates have to be fastened to a backup board so you can clamp them to your work. The Omnijig and Leigh systems have integral clamping; the Keller Jig requires you to provide the clamping. A clamping accessory is planned for in the near future, however.

The Keller template system is simplified by using all bearing-guided cutters. The dovetails and sockets always fit, regardless of the depth of cut. The depth is, of course, important to render the joints flush to the outside faces of the stock. The Keller system is primarily designed for fixed through dovetails on stock up to 1¼″ thick. It can also be used for compound angles, splines, box joints and knuckle joints. The templates are ½″ thick, and a phenolic laminate template is also available.

The fourth type of template system is the generic fixed-centered half-blind dovetail maker (Figure 7-6). It is primarily a small drawer- or box-making tool, although templates 16″ wide or wider are common. They include a clamping bar and sometimes a finer template comb for closer spacing of finer dovetails. Typically, the dovetail pin is 14° × ½″ wide and less than 7/16″ long. Material to 1″ in thickness can be routed in the jig. There are few adjustments, and with no prior experience the average woodworker can master the tool in one day. It can be fussy, however; most errors can be traced to poor material preparation, as squareness is critical in the use of this and all the other jigs.

Figure 7-4
The Keller Template System, in spite of its fixed template comb, is versatile. You must fasten the template to a backing board and provide your clamp to hold the work (photo supplied by Keller).

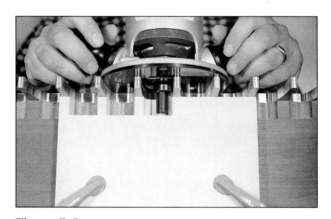

Figure 7-5
The pins are produced with a straight bit and a separate template. All the cuts are bearing-guided and as such are quite accurate (photo supplied by Keller).

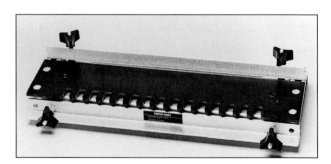

Figure 7-6
The Porter Cable fixed half-blind dovetail fixture is typical of the competition in this class. It has a modest clamping system and few adjustments. It is inexpensive (photo supplied by Porter Cable).

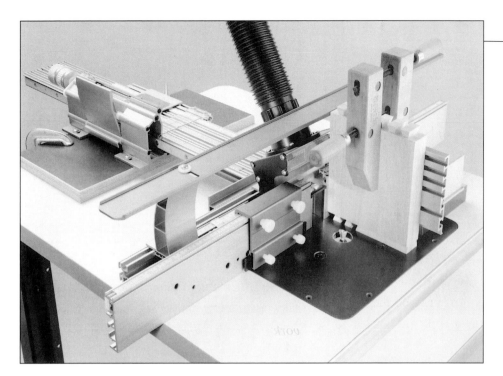

Figure 7-7
The fully loaded Incra System. The workpiece holder is in play, and the extension of the vertical fence, the vacuum system and the positioner are in view. Incra clearly has paid attention to detail (photo supplied by the Taylor Design Group).

INCRA JIG AND JOINTECH

Dovetail templates and hand routers have a lot of flexibility with respect to dovetail design, spacing and workpiece size. The stationary routing (tablework) fixtures are also quite flexible, but their range of work is not as extensive as the template and their cuttings are essentially restricted to boxes that you can get your arms or hands around. A blanket chest or gun cabinet is out of the question on the router table. The fixturing is not rated for medium- to large-scale projects.

There are only two contenders (as of this date) for table-fixtured fences, and they are quite similar and competitive (Figures 7-7 and 7-8). Basically, the table-rated dovetail fixtures provide a means to move the fence in a regular way so that each successive cut is a fixed distance from the one before it. A flat, sound router table and router are required to use either jig.

Since the fences can be positioned incrementally or continuously from any fixed point, all sorts of joints are possible. Box, finger joints and dovetails are typical examples, but there are also exotic cutting schedules that allow recutting

Figure 7-8
The Jointech IPM fence is also a table-only joinery system. Its fence moves continuously (no racks) and is indexed by a cursor. It is otherwise very similar to the Incra Jig (photo supplied by Jointech).

the joint and inlaying those cuts with other dovetails (Figures 7-9A–D).

Both of these jigs can be supplied with accessories that hold and stop the work. The Incra Jig uses a set of very accurate saw-tooth racks to position the fence; the Jointech IPM is positioned by referencing to a ruled tape and cursor. Both systems can also be used as precision fences for general table routing. For more information, see the List of Suppliers on page 139; for a neutral overview of all these contraptions, see *The New Router Handbook* by Pat Spielman (Sterling, 1993).

JIG SAFETY

1. Most of the cuttings with these jigs are full-depth, single-pass, power-hungry cuts. Consider pre-wasting to reduce tear-out, broken bits and kickback.

2. The table routings may require you to repeat the cuttings for a closer fit. Pay particular attention to which side of the cutting is recut. If the recut is cut on the right side of the cutter (fence side: work fed right to left), the cut is a climb cut and the work can be pulled from your hands or from the fixture unexpectedly.

3. Use at least 2½ hp for these heavy cuts, as a 1½ hp tool is underpowered and will heat up.

4. There are a lot of nuts, bolts, clamps, knobs, vises and miscellaneous hardware to track with these tools. You should write down a checklist so you don't forget any steps, as a slip here or there can ruin the work or cause injury.

Figure 7-9B
These box joints are typical of what can be produced from all of the aforementioned fixturing (photo supplied by Leigh).

Figure 7-9C
Rabbeted and unrabbeted half blind dovetail (photo supplied by Leigh).

Figure 7-9D
Through dovetails are evident from either the face or the side of this cabinet (photo supplied by Leigh).

CHAPTER EIGHT
Routing Lap Joints

LAP-JOINT BASICS

Lap joints are often identical excavations, cut with the same cutter, that overlay one another (Figures 8-1A and B). Their unhandedness and the fact that each facet of the joint is usually the same make them relatively easy to cut with all sorts of tools. By definition, they lap and therefore do not require any blind cutting. All the cuts are outside and usually square-edged.

Lap joints are especially friendly to routers, as the excavations are often very shallow and the jigging minimal. A 6 amp (1 hp) router has plenty of power to cut most laps. The cutters, short mill-to-pattern bits, are cheap, and ordinary straight bits and collars can also be used to cut the joint.

LAP-JOINT APPLICATIONS

The lap joint has a lot of applications. It can occur at the ends of a stick or anywhere in between. The joint can be at any angle (Figures 8-2A and B), and the workpieces can have the same or unequal thicknesses and widths. It can taper or have straight, parallel sides. The end laps on the edges of the stock can be at 90° or any other angle (Figure 8-3). The fraction of

Figures 8-1A and B
Each half of the end half lap is identical. The setup to cut the joint, the cutter and the depths of cuts are the same for each member.

Figure 8-4

In this arbitrary cross-lap the top piece is unjointed. This might be okay for joining sawhorse legs on site.

Figures 8-2A and B

Laps are the simplest joints to use to make triangles. Imagine trying to get all the angles correct for this sample on the table saw.

Figure 8-5

This lap is blind-ended. I made it with a template. The rosewood has to be lapped to hide its end grain.

Figure 8-3

The edges of this lap are at 14°. The glue-up process is much easier when the edges are at an angle.

Figure 8-6

Mortising this relatively thin piece of wide stock is not as practical as lapping.

thickness lapped can vary from nothing to more than half (Figure 8-4). The joint can run through or stop short of the edge (Figure 8-5). The thickness of material removed is so modest and the setup so trivial that this joint may indeed be the

sleeping giant in the forest of joinery.

Assemblies where the lap may be of benefit include frames, doors, leg-and-rail construction and connections where the width of the stock is much greater than the thickness (Figure 8-6).

CUTTING AN END LAP

The best way to cut an end lap is with the fixture used for cutting two-faced tenons on the flat (chapter four). You should study that jig and size it for your needs. Use a fixed-base router with an offset or oversize subbase of some sort so that the router won't dip into the window and spoil the cut. The most troublesome part of routing the joint is keeping the router flat. With an offset subbase and plenty of template, you'll have no problems.

I think the best cutter for cuttings less than ½″ deep is the PRC TA-170 (see the List of Suppliers on page 139); for cuttings from ⅜″ to ¾″ a Jesada 811-127B or equivalent should be used. For half laps where the sticks are of equal thickness but any width, follow the steps below.

STEP 1   Collet up the TA-170 and set it to a depth equal to the thickness of the template plus one-half the thickness of the stock.

STEP 2   Lay one stick across the other and knife a line along its edge (Figure 8-7).

Figure 8-7

A knife line is much skinnier than a pencil line, and if your lap setup is correctly indexed, you'll have less surface tear-out as the fibers are pre-severed here.

STEP 3   Clamp the work in the jig and rout as you would for a two-faced tenon. The knife line should line up with the working edge of the template (Figure 8-8).

STEP 4   Now lap this stick flush over the end of the other and knife-scribe along its edge.

STEP 5   Clamp this stick in the jig with its knife line along the working edge of the template and rout it to half thickness. This completes the cutting.

Figure 8-8

The knife line is on the cut line of the template and the cut is in progress. The work is clamped from the underside of the template so there is nothing fouling the footway of the router.

CUTTING THE CROSS LAP

There are a lot of ways to cut a cross lap, but by far the most flexible way is to use two short right-angle templates. The process is quite simple. Let's assume the work is of equal thickness but any width. If you lap and clamp one piece over the other and trap it between the two 90° templates, you're halfway there. Clamp the templates down, remove the work between them and rout out the space to complete the joint.

STEP 1   Locate the work against one of the templates as shown in Figure 8-9, and clamp the template down.

STEP 2   Now put a dollar bill between the other side of the stock and the right-hand template and clamp it in place. (Since the cutter is slightly smaller in diameter than the ½″ bearing on its shank, the dollar spacer will help compensate (Figure 8-9).

Figure 8-10
The area has been pre-routed with a collar and nearly routed to net with the pattern bit (TA-170).

STEP 3   Remove the work and set the depth of the cutter to cut to one-half thickness. Rout out the space defined by the two templates (Figure 8-10).

STEP 4   Insert the work in the excavation and set and clamp the templates plus a dollar bill against the routed piece, just as you did in step 2.

STEP 5   Now rout out that space (Figure 8-11).

Figure 8-9
For 90° positioning of the work use a 90° template. Crimp the work firmly between the two templates as you clamp them. Nothing can squiggle. Make sure of that before extracting the work and your money.

Figure 8-11
The second half of the cut has been routed. The most likely site for tear-out is free of tear-out because I clamped a scrap stick near that corner to press on the side grain.

Figures 8-12A and B

(Left; above) Lapping on edge is also common. Sometimes these cuttings, if only cut on-edge, are called cogged, bridled *or* halved.

MAKING THE SHELF BRACE

I made this shelf-brace triangle using the same technique. Note that one piece is routed on edge and the other, much wider piece (the hypotenuse) is unrouted (Figures 8-12A and B).

A NO-MORTISE MORTISE

Often I just can't find sticks big enough for legs on benches and such, so I have to glue them up from thinner stock. Before I glue the parts of the legs together, I may rout out a pair of spaces for the rails (Figure 8-13). Now when I glue the parts together, I can put a scrap rail in the mortise to keep the parts from squirming all over the place. The resulting mortise is really cool, as it is through, square-cornered and a cinch to rout (Figure 8-14).

Figure 8-13

This leg assembly is slightly misaligned so you can sense the separateness of the two pieces.

Figure 8-14

A scrap rail in the halvings simplifies glue-up. Without it the work squirms all over the place.

CHAPTER NINE
Routing Glue Joints

GLUE-JOINT BASICS

Glue-joint cutters were and still are part of the molder-and-shaper cutter inventories. Before the shaper, glue joints and other interlocking joinery were done by hand with the appropriate cutter blade and a hand plane. Transferring these designs into router bits is a relatively recent phenomenon.

Most glue-joint cutters are not symmetric and, as such, their correct depths of cut (fence and/or cutter height) are unknown until the full depth of cut is achieved. This is unlike cutting tongues and grooves, where either the slot width or the tongue thickness can be correctly accounted for before the final east-west fence position is selected. This won't be particularly problematic for you because I've designed a modified cutting schedule that will simplify the process. For each of the three cuttings we'll do, the strategy is a little different, but relatively easy nonetheless.

Glue joints, unlike other edge joints, have charisma because they are so often seen in production applications unavailable to the ordinary woodworker. There is a certain envy associated with the pleasant, professional look of processes beyond our capabilities. My students always ask me about glue joints and how to do them.

Figure 9-1
Glue joints are industrial art. Their design is minimal, exact and determinate. The first time you see a cutter you know what it's for. You can join edge to edge, edge to face or end grain to face grain with a glue joint cutter.

A glue joint is a very effective means of registering boards and locking them to one another in thickness. These joints offer a substantial additional glue line and, due to the strange asymmetry (unequal halves of profile) of the cutters, they can cut both sides of the joint at one depth of cut, a decided advantage over many joinery schemes. Moreover, they can joint and profile in one step.

EDGE-TO-EDGE GLUE JOINTING

Edge-to-edge glue joints are best done on the router table with at least a 2 hp motor. The initial and final adjustments should be done on equal-thickness scrap material, as there is no way to correctly set the depths of cut on the first try. The material removal is so great that as a rule it should be done in two steps, so a reproducible means of setting the final fence position is critical (Figure 9-2).

Some glue-joint cutters require a full-thickness cut. You must determine that from your supplier. If a full-thickness cut is required, an offset outfeed fence will be necessary. And incidentally, since the cutter is ground for a full thickness, you may wish to offset the fence anyway and joint and profile in one step (Figure 9-3).

Ordinary glue-joint cutters will join material from approximately $^{11}/_{16}$″ to $1^{1}/_{4}$″ thick. The T&G process we explored previously, however, is more accommodating to a wide array of thicknesses, and the shoulders of the tongue can always be cut to the correct proportion of overall thickness (usually equal to two-thirds). This is not the case with glue-joint cutters. You can center the profile, but the shoulders will have to vary as the work thickness varies (Figure 9-4). Nonetheless, the glue-joint cutter has its place, and since each cut is the same on each piece of stock, the system can be quite efficient.

Setup and Calibration

The easiest way to set the correct width of cut (left-right) is with an offset outfeed fence. If you take (cut) a full width profile plus a little, you have met the fence setting requirement. If you take less than a full profile (leaving some of the material uncut), you won't know if you've taken

Figure 9-2

My fence can pivot back to the pre-set adjuster. That makes it very easy to repeat a setting.

Figure 9-3

With an adjustable outfeed fence like this one you can joint and profile in one pass (workpiece half-milled). This was, incidentally, the original intent of these cutters. Any cutter used on the router table that cuts full thickness, can, indeed, joint as well as profile in one pass.

enough material or not. Taking more than a profile simplifies that part of the setup and joints the stock as well.

The correct vertical center line (north-south) position of the cutter can be ignored or painstakingly accounted for before the cutting run begins. It is best to center the cutter as close as is practical, but hitting dead center isn't essential. If you run a 1′ sample of profile and cut 2″ or 3″ off of it and compare the cutoff to the rest of the sample, you can discern and measure the centeredness (Figure 9-5). If you miss it by less than ¹⁄₁₆″, leave it alone. When you're ready to mill the adjacent boards, change the depth to account for any displacement.

The vertical depth of cut is probably the most bothersome of all routing endeavors. Trying to find the exact center line of any profile is much harder to do than making one arbitrary cut on half the stock and then making a second depth change for the rest of the boards. The reason for this is simple enough: If you're trying to hit the center line, any change in depth applies to both mating sticks simultaneously. So a ¹⁄₆₄″ change in net depth of cut is a ¹⁄₃₂″ change to the pair. If you're only concerned with making a depth change on one stick, then all of the net change applies only to that stick, not to the pair. Adjusting in this fashion is half as sensitive as trying to hit the center line.

Figure 9-4

The cutting on the left has a nice proportion of shoulder (straight section) to pin and notch. The much thinner profile on the right has very little shoulder. The minimum should be ¹⁄₈″.

Figure 9-5

I've cut off a 3″ piece and compared it to the rest of the sample. The up/down readjustment is equal to half of the displacement. If the faces miss alignment by ¹⁄₈″ then change the depth of cut by ¹⁄₁₆″.

PRODUCTION GLUE JOINTS

The system is somewhat cumbersome, as it is a scaled-down version of a production shaper process. The asymmetry of the joint is confusing but interesting. If the cutter height could be centered easily and if router motors were powerful enough, the process could be done a lot more easily. For the short run it is permissible to find the exact center of the profile and then joint and profile in one pass. This is how it's done in production. If you like the process, do a lot of cabinetmaking, and intend to join most of your material this way, you should consider a shaper.

Cutting an Edge-to-Edge Glue Joint

Now that you have some background, let's cut a sample edge-to-edge joint. We'll make the following three assumptions: First, we'll ignore the exact center line of the cutter; second, the cut will be made in two steps (since taking a full profile in one pass is too much work); and third, each member of a joint will be cut with the opposite face down on the router table.

STEP 1   Prepare your material in the usual way and assemble your planks in the order you'd like to glue them up. Indicate the face side of the stock and indicate which face of the board is against the table for which edge. As a rule, the most orderly way to lay this out is to cut each edge of the same board from opposite faces (Figure 9-6).

STEP 2   Position the vertical depth of the cutter to cut at or near its center line (Figure 9-7).

Figure 9-7

The straight sections of the cutter are about as equal as I can eyeball on the work.

STEP 3   Mill all the common edges (e.g., those that are face-down-only cuts) at approximately one-half the final left-right depth of cut, or about ⅛″.

STEP 4   Take the final pass on those boards. Position the fence to take .005″ to .010″ more than one profile (Figure 9-8). A

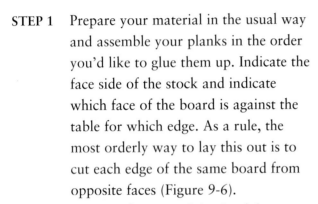

Figure 9-6

This is an end view of an ensemble of boards to be glue-jointed. The big arrow points to the face and the number inside it indicates its position in order from left to right. The arrows at each joint indicate which side of the board goes face down on the router table for that particular cut.

Figure 9-8

The bottom of the cutter is just beyond the infeed-fence setting. With the straightedge against the cutter, I can insert a 10-mil feeler gauge and adjust the outfeed fence parallel and 10 mils further out than the infeed fence.

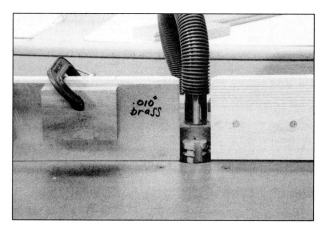

Figure 9-9
If you don't have a split fence, buy some junkyard sheet metal (.010" brass or aluminum) and clamp it to the outfeed side of the fence.

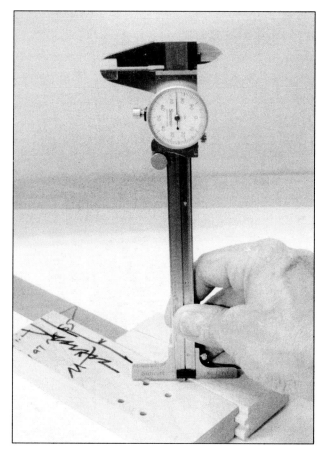

Figure 9-10
The dial caliper with its depth accessory measures the difference accurately. Raise or lower the cutter by the amount read off the caliper so the next cut evens out the fit.

split fence is the easiest way to do this. The outfeed fence has to be adjusted outward to receive the completely profiled edge. If you don't have a split fence, buy some junkyard sheet metal (.010" brass or aluminum) and clamp it to the outfeed side of the fence (Figure 9-9).

STEP 5 Take any two sticks and fit them together. Measure the displacement at the surface (Figure 9-10). The cutter height must be changed by this amount.

STEP 6 Cut 10" or more of equal-thickness scrap material without changing the fence setting in step 4. The surfaces should meet. If they don't, adjust the cutter height until they do.

STEP 7 Reduce the depth of cut to about ⅛" and realign the fences (Figures 9-11A and B). Cut all the unmilled edges with their appropriate faces down on the table.

STEP 8 Set the fences back to the condition in step 4 and mill the final pass. This completes the cutting.

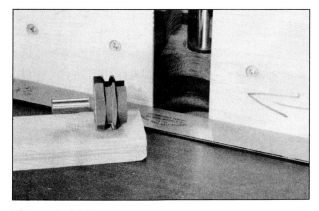

Figure 9-11A
The fences are in-line for this cut since some of the profile is uncut. I set the fences with a Bridge City straightedge.

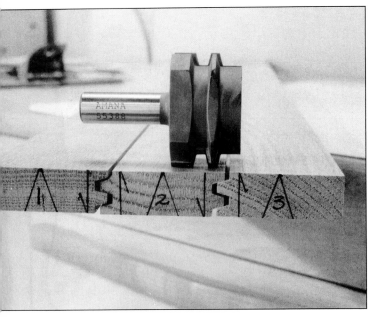

Figure 9-11B

This joint is quite photogenic. The cutter is Amana 55388. Glue-up is easy as all the boards lock up quite nicely.

EDGE-TO-FACE GLUE JOINERY

Long-grain face-to-edge joints are valuable because they provide a means for joining boards into *L*-sections. *L*-sections are evident in furniture legs, backsplashes on counter tops and ledger assemblies for bed rails, and countless examples can be found in jigs, fixtures and fences (Figure 9-12). This joint is best cut from a cutter like this excellent Whiteside Machine Company 3352 (Figure 9-13). The joint is cut only on the router table. If the depth of cut is centered on the edge of the work, both cuts can be made at the same fence and cutter settings. One piece is cut on edge, and the other is cut face down on the table.

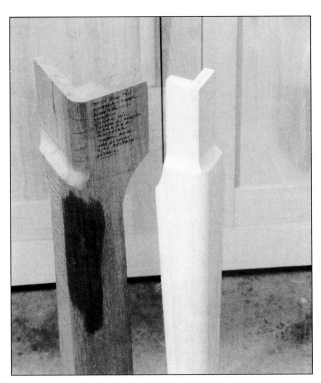

Figure 9-12

These legs were a first guess at a design for a client's dinner table. Rather than create the thing from a solid 4"-square chunk of a log, I made it from a glue-jointed L-section.

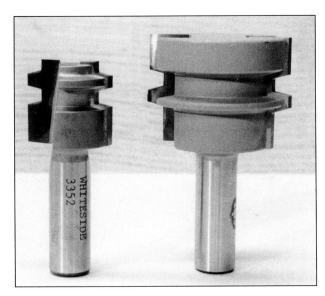

Figure 9-13

A glue joint cutter must have its major diameter next to the shank for it to work in an edge-to-face-grain connection. The cutter on the right is only for edge work. The Whiteside 3352 is on the left.

Cutting the Edge-to-Face Glue Joint

STEP 1 Adjust the cutter height so it's approximately centered on the stock (Figure 9-14).

STEP 2 Set the fence to cut to, but no deeper than, the bottom of the notch. The bottom of the notch is the minimum diameter of the profile (Figure 9-15).

STEP 3 Rout a 12″ length of profile and cut a 3″ piece off one end. Nest the cutoff in the 9″ piece. If the surfaces don't meet, measure the displacement and divide that number by two.

STEP 4 Change the north-south cutter depth by the amount determined in step 3 and repeat step 3 until the surfaces are coincident (even).

STEP 5 Rout the edge of your boards. Make no changes and rout the profile on the faces of the boards that require it (Figures 9-16A and B).

If you have a long run of material to machine, do it in stages.

Figure 9-15
The straight section beyond the pin on the cutter should do no cutting. The sample on the left has been cut too deeply. The depth of cut is just right on the other sample.

Figure 9-16A
My fence is high enough to support stock on edge. For safety's sake, your fence height should be greater than half the width of your boards.

Figure 9-16B
The complete joint.

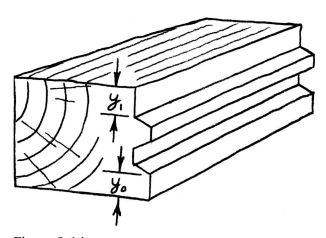

Figure 9-14
If the straight section (on the stock) above the pin is equal in height to the straight section below the notch, the cut is centered ($Y_0 = Y_1$).

DRAWER LOCK GLUE JOINT

The drawer lock glue joint is an excellent drawer joint. The key ingredient of any good joint is fit. Perfectly hewn pins and tails do not a perfect dovetail make: The fit is just as important as the cuttings, and the drawer joint is no exception. However, since all components (sides, fronts and backs) are cut from the same cutter, the fit is greatly simplified.

For the short run (less than twenty-five drawers), the joint should be cut with the hand router. Router-table work will require sophisticated fixturing, and for the short run it's just not worth the trouble. The hand router and template are the tools of choice here. You'll need the jig for on-end cuts, a Whiteside 3352 glue-joint cutter, a 1⅛"-diameter bearing with a ½" bore (Whiteside B-11 or equivalent), some Loctite, an offset router subbase and a ¾"-thick right-angle template (Figure 9-17). (A ½" stop collar such as Jesada's 541-002 can substitute for the Loctite.)

Figure 9-17
This is all you'll need for a drawer-lock joint. The bearing is glued on the cutter shank with Locktite brand methacrylic ester no. 271. The bearing is ⅛" larger in diameter than the cutter. A collar, shown, can also keep the bearing in place.

Figure 9-18
This sample connection is for drawers with ½"-thick steel slides. It could be flush if the drawer were carried on a drawer blade.

Cutting the Drawer Joint

The drawer front or back is cut with the work flat and the template clamped on top of it. The lateral depth of cut is arbitrary but should be at least as deep as the drawer side is thick (Figure 9-18). The sides of the drawers are cut while fixed and indexed on-end in the jig for end cuts (hereafter called the *beam*). The same ¾"-thick template is used to limit the left-right depth of cut. This joint has only one simplification factor and that is on this side cut. The east-west depth of cut is correct only when there is no bottom cutting. It's not much of a hedge, but it is a good indicator nonetheless. The correct depth of cut is determined by cutting into sample stock, producing some bottom cutting and then repositioning the template to the right by the amount the bottom of the cutter has cut into the stock. Let's look at the procedure.

STEP 1   Place the front flat on the beam (or bench) and position the template one drawer side thickness plus ½" plus ⁷⁄₃₂" from the end. The ½" is for a ½"-thick drawer slide, if you want flush sides, subtract ½" from the measurement (Figure 9-19).

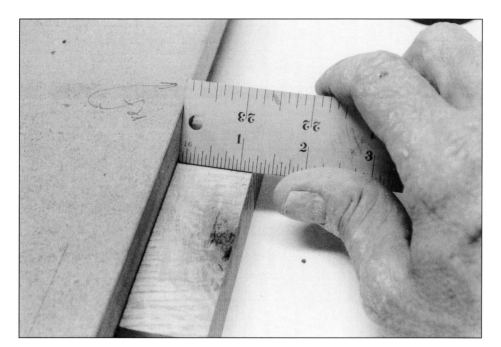

Figure 9-19

The position of the template is a direct measurement to the end of stock. The squareness of your work and of the template are critical. If either is amiss the cutting will reflect that error.

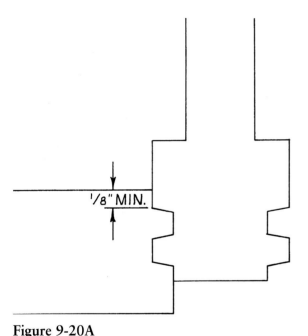

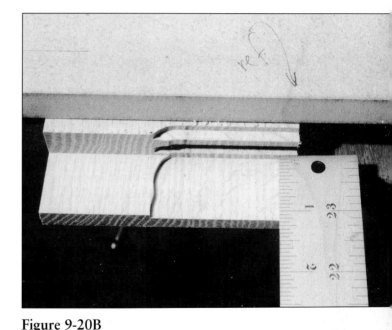

Figure 9-20A

Set the cutter so at least ⅛" of shoulder is cut (⁹⁄₁₆" overall minimum). If the flatland is wider than ⅜" you should saw or pre-rabbet away at least 80 or 90 percent of it.

Figure 9-20B

I have pre-wasted for this cut. I've left some of the area uncut by the glue jointer. The bulk of the cut was done with a 1¼" O.D. collar and ¾" (cutting diameter) straight bit.

STEP 2 Set the cutter depth for at least an ⅛" of shoulder and rout left to right. If the flatland is greater than ⅜", do some pre-wasting (Figures 9-20A and B).

STEP 3 Index some equal-thickness (equal to thickness of side) scrap vertically on the beam and position the template about ¼" in from the face of the stock.

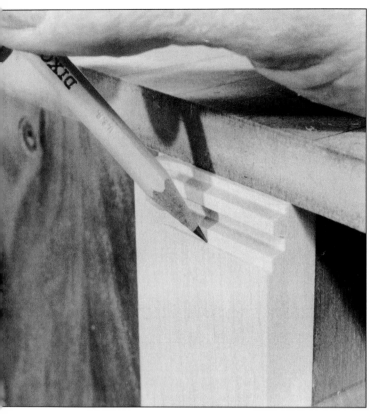

Figure 9-21

The work is indexed against the bottom of the template, and the bottom of the cutter has cut into the side of the stock. There is less than ⅛" of shoulder above the pin.

Set the cutter depth so there is less than ⅛" of shoulder above the pin, and rout the profile (Figure 9-21).

STEP 4   Check the fit with the front. The end of the side should "kiss" the back side of the drawer front (Figure 9-22).

STEP 5   Repeat the cut on scrap. Lower the cutter the amount of the gap in step 4 and slide the template to the right by the same amount the bottom of the cutter cut into the side. The side cut should be such that there is no side cutting produced by the cutter below its pin (Figures 9-23A and B).

Figure 9-22

There should be no gap between the end of the side and the back of the front. The feeler gauge is .015", so lower the cutter by ¹⁄₆₄". The template should also be moved to the right the same amount the bottom of the cutter cut into the side.

Figure 9-23A

The joint fits perfectly now. The straight section of the cutter below the pin should not cut into the sides.

Figure 9-23B

This walnut/oak sample is for a flush connection.

SMALL CABINETS AND GLUE JOINTS

Small cabinets, such as shallow bookcases, can be joined in much the same way. The strength of the joint is derived largely from the glue interface. If the joint is cut well, glued sufficiently and clamped squarely, the maximum pull-strength of the joint can be realized. This joint in a cabinet can be quite serviceable if the cabinet is on a stand or sits directly on the floor. If the cabinet is wall-hung, on the other hand, the stresses on the bottom joints are constant (unlike a resting drawer), and if the whole load of the cabinet is on the bottom joints they should be re-inforced (Figures 9-24A and B).

Glue joinery is entirely machine work and as such may not appeal to some woodworkers. For me, the glue-joint cutter is like commercial art. It can be appealing. It's certainly a challenge and lends itself well to repetition, but it'll never be much more than Warhol's Campbell's Soup cans.

Figures 9-24A and B
I made this storage box with a glue-joint cutter. There are through dowels in it for reinforcement. The door was also glue-jointed!

CHAPTER TEN

Splining With a Router

SPLINE BASICS

Routing for splines is easier than routing tongues and grooves. The slot for the spline is router-cut on the table from the common faces of the work, and the spline stock is a jointer/planer/band saw process. Splines can usually be used where tongues and grooves are called for. I use them when a little decoration is needed or when tongue cutting (for a T&G joint) is difficult or impractical (Figure 10-1).

Using a Slotting Bit

Slotters are pretty neat router tools. Their radial design is like that of a saw blade and, as such, their cutting action is very efficient. I can't put a number on it, but I can give you some idea of just how efficient they are. A 1 hp router, in one pass, can (with a slotter) cut a ¼″ wide by ½″ deep slot without much ado. A ¼″-diameter straight bit cutting ½″ deep will either stall the router or break the bit. If you're fortunate enough not to do either, you will burn the bit to death in less than 1′ of stock.

Slotting, the essential cutting process for splines, should be done on the router table whenever possible. Slotters are generally large-diameter tools, and if used in a hand router they are used at risk (Figure 10-2). Part of the risk is related to the cutter engagement with the work. A slotter is a strong tool and cuts deep, but only if the spindle is perpendicular to the face of the stock. If the work rocks or the router tilts, the plate the teeth are welded to starts to bend. Once this occurs the slot is widened, kickback can occur and the whole assembly can be pulled from the collet—a disaster.

Figure 10-1

In a major glue-up, such as this 11′ × 22″ slab, the ends of the boards have to be registered (joined) or they slide all over during assembly. A spline is an easy solution. The splines will also keep the sticks from creeping after glue-up.

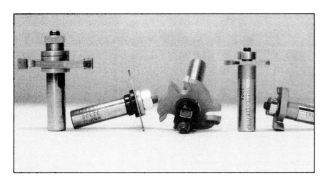

Figure 10-2

The thickest production-made wing slotter is ⁹⁄₃₂" (a PRC product). The thinnest is WKW's .050" three-wing tool. Slotters are supplied in two, three and four wings depending on usage and manufacturing. Smaller diameter slotters like the Whiteside one-piece tools (right) are really specialized rabbeters that cut like slotters. They are available in thicknesses (cutter lengths) to ³⁄₄" and beyond.

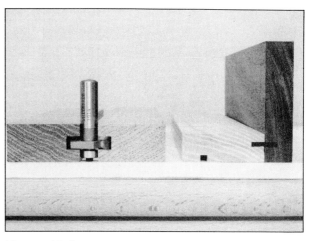

Figure 10-3

The slots on the pair of sticks on the left have been centered. The slotter is thinner than the slot. The face-to-edge assembly (right) was cut with only one fence and cutter depth position. This substantially simplifies the cutting schedule.

A spline should be at least ½" to ³⁄₄" wide. A slot that deep requires a large-diameter tool, and large-diameter tools are dangerous and scary when used with a hand router. Use the router table whenever possible.

SLOTTING FOR SPLINES

The slotting process is unremarkable. The procedure is the same as that used in the groove-making step when making the T&G. The slot can be rendered centered if the cuttings are done with each face of the board down on the table. The centeredness can also be ignored as long as the slotting is done with only the face side down on each board. Cutting from each side of the stick not only centers the slot, but also gives you the option of widening it should you so desire. If you are slotting the face of one stick and the edge of another, you should cut only one slotter width (Figure 10-3).

Cutting a Slot

STEP 1   Prepare your material in the usual way. Keep in mind that the mating edges and faces of your stock are produced from the saw, planer and jointer, and not from a router bit like they would be in a glue joint or tongue and groove.

Figure 10-4

My fence has some slots in it to reduce the contact with the work. Less contact means easier travel.

STEP 2 Set the fence and cutter height and slot all the material from the common face.

STEP 3 For edge-to-face splines, don't bother to center the edge piece slot by flipping the board over and routing twice.

STEP 4 For edge-to-face slots, use a fence high enough to safely support your stock on edge (Figure 10-4).

MAKING SPLINES

There must be a million ways to make spline stock—and you can buy it. (The Woodworkers' Store sells ⅛″ and ¼″-thick stock.) For example, you can rip it on the table saw or band saw and sand it. I tried a few sawing techniques and I tried some store-bought stuff—neither of which I liked. With my schedule you can safely make your own out of matching species or special exotic contrasting material.

STEP 1 Carefully measure the slot depth, double it and subtract .003″ to .005″. This number will be the thickness you are to mill to. (**Note:** Working in thousandths of an inch may seem crazy in woodworking, but it's really quite easy to do. A dial caliper will keep things under control.)

STEP 2 Joint some very straight-grained material and thickness it to the number derived in step 1. Joint both edges of the board.

STEP 3 Measure the width of the slot (which may well be the thickness of the slotter you used). Band saw some slices off each edge of the board in step 2. These cuttings should be about ¼″ thicker than the slot.

STEP 4 Plane the cuttings in step 3 to a slip fit for your slots (Figures 10-5 and 10-6). If your spline stock is fragile (less than ³⁄₁₆″ thick) or cut from wavy-grained material, it can explode in the planer—but it's relatively harmless if it does. Material under ³⁄₁₆″ should probably be thickness-sanded. Some daredevils I've talked to think nothing of table-sawing skinny stock. If you must saw, use the appropriate push sticks and hold-downs.

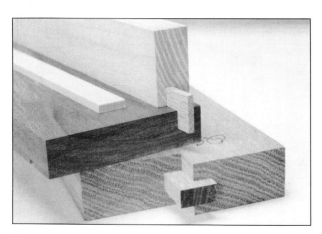

Figure 10-5
Your splines should slip into the slot. If they are too loose you'll lose registration and if they're too tight you'll have a terrible time clamping.

Figure 10-6
I've glued sandpaper to an MDF carrier for traction. Feeding at 10° to 20° allows more blade and roller on the spline so it has less chance to run amok.

Gluing Splines

The gluing process is straightforward; however, splines are strange. They suck up a lot of glue and get fat. Do some testing of glue application on scrap before assembly. Good, close spline joinery can jam if you're too sloppy about glue application and forgetful of time.

END SPLINING

The ends of these boards were splined with a hand router and bearing-guided slotter (Figure 10-7). I used two splines in this walnut slab. The boards have stayed flat for more than ten years. The ends of the boards in Figure 10-8 were glue-jointed, but I camouflaged the joint with two splines. The splines had a termination mishap (the ends) and I camouflaged that problem with some walnut dowels.

Splines are also useful to join two boards in a scarf. A *scarf* is board-lengthening joinery. The boards are cut on a bias, slotted, and splined for registration (Figure 10-9).

Figure 10-7
I used two splines in this walnut slab. The boards have stayed flat for more than ten years.

Figure 10-8
You can use splines for more than just joinery.

Figure 10-9
The color and figure are so closely matched in this scarf that you can't see the joint line; I've drawn it in for clarity.

CHAPTER ELEVEN
Miscellaneous and Decorative Joints

Routed joints, for the most part, are strong enough on their own not to require any reinforcement or subsequent locking. There are, of course, instances where there is simply not enough power nor cutters made to produce a joint of sufficient scale from a router. Timber framing, castle entryway doors, conference tables, and church and architectural millwork are examples that come to mind. Moreover, a routed joint may well meet the standards of ordinary situations, but you might like a little decoration or insurance against a failure. After all, you might have to make something for a public library, nursery or county park, and that stuff can't fail.

Figure 11-2
This template has a lot of clamping face. Squareness is not critical; in fact, the cutter pathway off this template is 10° from perpendicular to offer more dovetail pin engagement. The work is sandwiched between two pieces of scrap to prevent any tear-out.

In this chapter I'd like to explore some of the novelties I've invented. Some of the cuttings are strictly decorative, some essential, some certainly unusual and probably all unexpected.

LOCKING A LAP WITH A DOVETAIL PIN

Figure 11-1
A lap is strong because of its glue interface area. A dovetail pin or pins can decorate it and lock it too.

An end lap is a substantial joint in its own right but it has no interlock. Without glue it can't hold itself together. Screws aren't much help either because laps are so thin there can't be much thread engagement. A well-placed through dovetail pin can offer some interlock and a little decoration. You can use pins on one or both edges of the lap (Figure 11-1).

STEP 1   Make your lap in the usual way and glue it up.

STEP 2   Hold the work on edge and clamp it between two pieces of backup stock.

STEP 3   Use a short right- or angled-angle template and clamp it across your sandwich (Figure 11-2).

STEP 4   Use two routers with the same-diameter collar guides. Let one router pre-plow the slot with a straight bit, and let the other router follow the plow with the dovetail bit. Allow only one cutter-width pass of the dovetail. The collars and cutters are your choice, as are the location of the template and number of ways (Figure 11-3).

STEP 5   Select your dovetail stock and rout long-grain dovetail pins on the router table. Let the height of the dovetail be at least one band saw kerf greater than the depth of the way (Figure 11-4).

STEP 6   Cut off short lengths, just a little longer than the thickness of the lap. Wet the socket and the pin generously with glue. Insert the pins (Figure 11-5).

STEP 7   Band saw or hand saw off the waste and sand flush (Figure 11-6).

Figure 11-3
I cut two small dovetail ways here using Jesada 818-097. Note how clean the entry and exit ways are.

Figure 11-4
Rout a centered pin on stock wide enough to hold safely on edge. Let the fit be snug, but no hammer fits, knocking or rocking.

Figure 11-5
I don't usually get too sloppy with glue. But dovetails do jam and a lot of glue allows for an easier fit in this case. No clamping is necessary.

Figure 11-6
The finished reinforced joint. Note that I dovetailed the half lap itself. The lap assembly is a lot easier if you can jam one of the pieces into a dovetail shoulder like this.

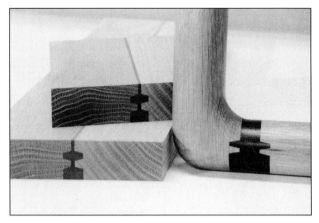

Figure 11-7
The joint we're going to do is on the left. The more radical cut on the right uses roughly the same schedule but after the joinery all the corners are rounded.

A PIN-STRIPED GLUE JOINT

This joint (Figure 11-7) is strictly decorative and as such should be done with somewhat contrasting stock. For me, black walnut on *Acer alba* (maple) is just too bright. Cherry on walnut is more my style. Start by centering the cutter. If the cutter is not centered, it'll take forever to make the adjustments for each step.

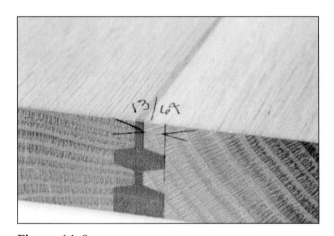

Figure 11-8
The decorator stock projects about $^{13}/_{64}$" beyond the glue line for a $^3/_{64}$" stripe using the Amana 55388 cutter. You could also taper the cut so the stripe would go to zero on one end.

STEP 1   Glue-joint your panel stock and a 2" width of your decorative stock. Glue these two pieces together.

STEP 2   I like my stripes about $^3/_{64}$" in width. If you agree, rip the glue up so $^{13}/_{64}$" of decorative stock resides beyond the glue line on the face side (Figure 11-8).

STEP 3   Glue-joint the decorator stock face side down, and continue cutting your panel stock in the usual way. The glue-up should have the skinny stripe on top (Figure 11-9).

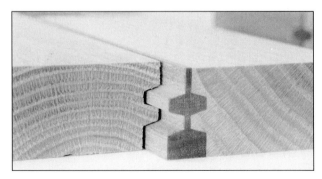

Figure 11-9
The joint is also shown loose for clarity.

MENDING A TWO-RAIL CENTER-LEG ASSEMBLY

There may come a time when you're building a table so long that you'll need a center leg to support it. If two rails are joined to one center leg, there may not be enough material left in the leg for a serviceable joint. The joint then needs to be mended or strengthened. A notched, essentially lapped stick, spanning both rails and legs, will add strength (Figure 11-10). The mending connector can be glued and/or screwed. If the connector is on the show face, it can be screwed on from the inside.

STEP 1   Cut the mending plate to size. For heavy-duty stuff I like at least 8″ to 10″ of material stuck to each rail.

STEP 2   Use scrap from the leg to set up for a midlap on the mending plate (Figure 11-11).

STEP 3   If the leg and rails are flush on the mending-plate surface, no lap is required. If not, cut the lap the same depth as the rails are from the face of the leg (Figure 11-12).

STEP 4   I always decorate my splices a bit. A straight fat stick, although entirely acceptable, is simply too mud-fence ugly for me (Figure 11-13).

Figure 11-10
The mending stick can be as big as you like to support any practical load.

Figure 11-12
The leg/rails are ⅛″ from the face of the leg, so cut the lap ⅛″ deep.

Figure 11-11
The setup is the same for any square cross-grain lap.

Figure 11-13
I did a little bandsawing and I finished the ogee on the edge sander.

STILE AND RAIL MENDING

Small doors that are mortised and tenoned by routers (Figures 11-14A and B) can be compromised. Skinny rails (⅝″ to ⅞″ thick) can be tenoned adequately since they're outside cuts. Deep, narrow, proportionally correct mortises in stiles are a problem. There are no cutters long enough or stiff enough to cut much deeper than 1″. (The mortise width on skinny stock should be around ³⁄₁₆″ to ¼″.) Consequently, rail-and-stile router-cut mortises and tenons can be a compromise. I will concede, however, that skinny lightweight doors should not be expected to encounter much stress, and for the most part shallow sliding dovetails or tenons are acceptable.

If you use a mending plate, there are no compromises. Even very shallow tenons (½″ long or less) are acceptable when a bridge of material is screwed (and/or glued) across the stile and rail. The procedure to make such a plate differs little from the previous example. If the rail and stile are flush, simply screw on a plate. If they are not, like my example, then rout a little material away so the bridge nests across the joint evenly. Again, there is opportunity for styling the bridge, even if it's on the inside of the door (also see Figure 5-28, page 93).

Figures 11-14A and B
The bridge of material (I call it a mending plate; the Brits call it a fish plate) crosses the rail and stile. It can be styled, if you like, to act as a pull.

THE FINGER-JOINT CUTTER

Like the glue joint, the finger-joint cutter (Figure 11-15) is on loan from the shaper industry. It was designed to join stock end to end, industry's way of saving clear short stock. In production the systems work well, but they are sophisticated, powerful and very expensive. The router bit finger jointer is a good cutter, but don't expect it to go to work for you like a production tool. You must consider the bit a short-run, minimum-duty tool, but a useful one nonetheless.

The power requirements are enormous when compared to other router bits. By spacing the cutters and adjusting the cutter height, material from 7/16″ to about 1 3/8″ can be worked. The cutter's east-west depth of cut varies from manufacturer to manufacturer, but generally they take about 3/16″ to 1/4″ of material. Fully one-half the thickness of the work is wasted. So if you're milling a 1″-thick board at 1/4″ depth, 1/2″ × 1/4″ of stock is being removed. While edge-to-edge and end-to-edge cuttings are typical, the original intent of the tool was for end-grain to end-grain cuttings. End-grain cuttings take substantially more horsepower than long-grain cuts.

Using the Finger-Joint Cutter

Finger-joint cutters work about the same as glue-joint cutters: The same cut is produced on each side of the joint. If the cutter is centered on the stock, the same fence and cutter height positions are used for both halves of the joint. The tool consumes a lot of material, so the cutting should be in stages. To me, three equal cuts seems about right. The cutter engagement with the work is substantial. You must have a means of holding the work flat, as any rotation will spoil the cut and maybe kick back.

You must study the direction sheet that comes with each tool for the correct spacing, cutter height and fence settings. In general these tools are supplied with bearings, and the fence should be tangential (even) with the bearing. Obviously, the operation is strictly a table cut. Long-grain and long-grain–face-grain cuts are done just like glue joints (see chapter nine).

Figure 11-15

Finger-joint cutters are big power-hungry cutters. For their depth of cut they remove roughly half the stock in thickness.

Cutting End-Grain to End-Grain Finger Joints

STEP 1 Rout equal-thickness edge-grain scrap to calibrate the fence setting and cutter centeredness. Rout on top of a ⅜″-thick auxiliary MDF surface (Figure 11-16).

STEP 2 Cut two parallel pieces of ⅜″ MDF. One should be about 4½″ wide (for a 7″-wide miter gauge); the other should cover the rest of your router table. These panels will trap your miter gauge blade and keep its travel parallel to the fence (Figure 11-17).

STEP 3 Use a backup stick on the miter gauge and rout the end grain in stages. Try to divide the work into three equal cuts. Be sure that you can always get the final fence position to the same spot (Figure 11-18).

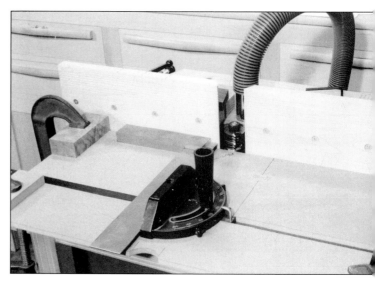

Figure 11-17

The MDF panels trap the miter gauge blade and maintain its travel parallel to the fence. The gauge must be 90° to the fence. Clamp the MDF panels to the table.

Figure 11-18

The end-grain cut is a very demanding cut. You must keep the stock flat and backed up so as to prevent tear-out.

Figure 11-16

The bearing is tangential to the fence and the vertical height has been centered. When the straight shoulder is equal in height to the uncut straight section the cutter is centered. I'm routing on ⅜″ MDF. (The auxiliary table surface material thickness is governed by the thickness of your miter gauge blade. The blade must be equal to or thinner than the MDF.)

DOUBLE TONGUE AND GROOVE FOR THICKNESS GLUING

Figure 11-19

Using principles of simple tongue-and-groove joinery, this interlocking joint prevents lateral slippage during clamping and produces straight, clear, thick stock from thin stock.

(Much of this section was originally published in the December 1994 issue of *Woodwork* on pages 54 and 55.)

I make more furniture with legs and rails than I do with glued-up panels or edged 4′ × 8′ sheet stock, and for making legs I prefer stock from 2″ to 2½″ square. Quality material in this thickness range is not very common where I live—if it is available, it's at a premium price, poorly dried (usually), in limited supply and in grades less than FAS, and it rarely has grain and figure consistent with that found in thinner stock. To get both the thickness and the quality I want, I build up a lamination of two pieces of 5/4 or 6/4 lumber. Material in this thickness range is readily available, relatively cheap, consistently dried and subject to much more user scrutiny than 10/4, 12/4 or 16/4.

In the past I've done a lot of thickness gluing by simply gluing together two jointed faces, but glue-up was a struggle and my re-sults were always inconsistent. I might get one side of the glue line to close here and there, but no matter how hard I tried, I could never get both glue lines tight. However, I've had good, consistent results with tongue-and-groove edge gluing, so on a lark I thought I'd try a similar joint and apply the same principles to face gluing. Lo, it worked—and way beyond my expectations, I might add. I now glue legs up to 2¾″ thick as a routine practice. I'm able to match grain and figure most of the time, and the glue lines are always gap-free. On occasion the glue lines are visible, however, but this is a result of poorly matched wood grain or color.

That aside, let's get to the process. Briefly, the joint is a shallow double tongue and groove that is symmetric about its center line. The mating pair is pre-milled to the same width, perhaps ⅛″ wider than finished size, and the joint is cut on the router table using only a ¼″ thick slotter and arbor (such as Amana slotter assembly 53410-1).

The stock must be flat, well squared to its edges, and the same width, but mating pieces needn't be the same thickness. The key to the process is its symmetry and centeredness. All the cuts are made with one edge on the router table for the first side of the cut, then flipped over 180° for the opposite side of the cut. This tactic automatically centers the joint within the workpiece.

The gluing process is facilitated with a thick caul the same width as the leg and clamped with C-clamps 3″ or 4″ apart along the center line. After the glue has cured, the legs are remilled square to finished dimensions.

The steps are as follows:

1. Mill 5/4 or 6/4 stock (including about two feet of scrap) square, true and to width. To achieve a centered glue line on the finished piece, part A should be milled ⅛″ thicker than part B. Note that each tongue and groove is approximately one-fifth of the total stock width (Figure 11-20).

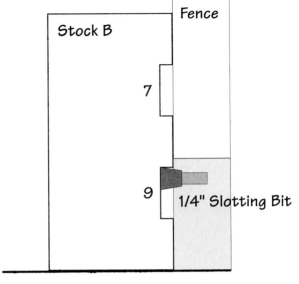

Figure 11-21

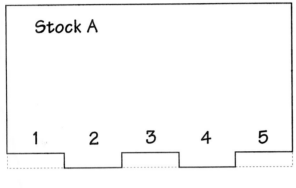

Figure 11-20

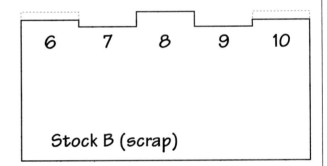

Figure 11-22

2. Cut about ⅛″ deep (with a ¼″ slotting bit) on Stock B as shown (Figure 11-21). A first pass begins Groove 7. Without changing any settings, flip the workpiece to cut Groove 9. Now, raise the cutter (less than ¼″) to widen Groove 7. Flip the stock to complete Groove 9.

3. On a scrap piece of Stock B, cut away enough of Projections 6 and 10 so that Projection 8 stands alone (Figure 11-22). This will serve as the test gauge for achieving the proper width of Groove 3.

4. Adjust the fence to increase the depth of cut by two to five thousandths (a paper thickness). Now, cut Groove 3 on a scrap piece of Stock A (Figure 11-23). Lowering the cutter as necessary, widen the groove until you produce a slip-fit onto Projection 8 from the scrap Stock B. (Remember to flip the workpiece at each bit setting to keep the cut automatically centered.) Once the cutter depth is adjusted to produce an acceptable fit, cut Groove 3 in all of Stock A.

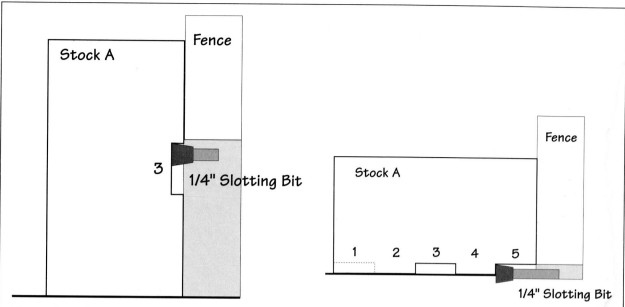

Figure 11-23

Figure 11-24

5. Cut rabbets 1 and 5 on Stock A as shown (Figure 11-24). Using Stock B as a gauge, adjust the depth of cut to make these rabbets a paper thickness shallower than cuts 7 and 9—this will prevent the assembly from bottoming out at glue-up. Adjust the fence so

Projections 2 and 4 fit into 7 and 9. Note that each edge is worked against the fence to ensure symmetry. Once the calibration cuts have been made on Stock A, cut rabbets 1 and 5 in all of Stock A.

LIST OF SUPPLIERS

Amana Tool Corp.
120 Carolyn Blvd.
Farmingdale, NY 11735
(800) 445-0077
A huge selection of wonderful router bits.

Bridge City Tool Works
1104 N.E. 28th Ave.
Portland, OR 97232
(800) 253-3332
Precision layout and metrology tools.

Bruss Fasteners
P.O. Box 88307
Grand Rapids, MI 49518-0307
(800) 563-0009
Hardware, T-nuts, scews, cross-dowels and
other specialty fasteners.

DeWalt Industrial Tool Co.
P.O. Box 158
625 Hanover Pike
Hampstead, MD 21074
(800) 4-DeWalt
Electric hand tools and plastic offset router
bases.

Eagle America
P.O. Box 1099
Chardon, OH 44024
One of the largest router bit selections in North
America.

Jesada Tools, Inc.
310 Mears Blvd.
Oldsmar, FL 34677
(813) 891-6160
Premier router bits and router offset subbases.

Terry Kirkpatrick
% Col. Joe Kirkpatrick, USMC/Ret.
551 Taylor St.
Vista, CA 92084
Artist/illustrator.

Microfence
11100 Cumpston St. #35
North Hollywood, CA 91601
(800) 480-6427
Nicely adjustable edge guides and circle cutter
pivots for most routers.

Paso Robles Carbide, Inc.
731-C Paso Robles St.
Paso Robles, CA 93446
(805) 238-6144
Router bits, including many of the longest,
largest-diameter and other parameters on the extreme end.

Patrick Warner
1427 Kenora St.
Escondido, CA 92027
(760) 747-2623; fax (760) 745-1753
Maker and supplier of the acrylic offset router
bases. Author of *Getting the Very Best From
Your Router*.

Popular Woodworking Magazine
1507 Dana Ave.
Cincinnati, OH 45207

Porter Cable Corp.
P.O. Box 2468
Jackson, TN 38302
(901) 668-8600
Routers, router accessories and other electric
hand tools.

Reid Tool Supply Co.
2265 Black Creek Rd.
Muskegon, MI 49444-2684
(800) 253-0421
Jig and fixture hardware of all sorts.

Ridge Carbide Tool Co.
595 New York Ave.
Lyndhurst, NJ 07071
(800) 443-0992
Sharpening of router bits.

The L.S. Starrett Co.
121 Crescent St.
Athol, MA 01331
Precision scales, calipers and layout tools, etc.

Ken Schroeder
3120 Gaewood Ct.
Alliance, OH 44601
(330) 821-7571
Photographic printing service and consulting.

W.L. Fuller, Inc.
P.O. Box 8767
7 Cypress St.
Warwick, RI 02888
(401) 467-2900
Router bits, drilling tools.

Wisconsin Knife Works
2505 Kennedy Dr.
Beloit, WI 53511
(608) 363-7888
Plunging and other router bits.

Whiteside Machine Co.
4506 Shook Rd.
Claremont, NC 28610
(800) 225-3982
Very competitive router bits; all American made.

Wolfcraft, Inc.
P.O. Box 687
1222 W. Ardmore Ave.
Itasca, IL 60143
(630) 773-4777
Supplies a nice spring clamp for temporary hold-fast, and many other tools.

Woodhaven
5323 W. Kimberly Rd.
Davenport, IA 52806
(800) 344-6657
Routing equipment.

Woodwork
P.O. Box 1529
Ross, CA 94957-9987
A magazine for all woodworkers.

Woodworkers' Store
4365 Willow Dr.
Medina, MN 55340
(800) 279-4441
Over 4,000 products including offset router bases.

INDEX